RECOVERING
FROM A
BROKEN HEART

RECOVERING FROM A BROKEN HEART

*A Companion Guide
for the Journey from
Suffering to Joyful Awareness*

PHILIP GOLABUK

1817

HARPER & ROW, PUBLISHERS, NEW YORK
CAMBRIDGE, PHILADELPHIA, SAN FRANCISCO
LONDON, MEXICO CITY, SÃO PAULO, SINGAPORE, SYDNEY

RECOVERING FROM A BROKEN HEART. Copyright © 1989 by Philip Golabuk. All rights reserved. Printed in the United States of America. No part of this book may be used or reproduced in any manner whatsoever without written permission except in the case of brief quotations embodied in critical articles and reviews. For information address Harper & Row, Publishers, Inc., 10 East 53rd Street, New York, N.Y. 10022. Published simultaneously in Canada by Fitzhenry & Whiteside Limited, Toronto.

FIRST EDITION

Designed by: Cassandra J. Pappas

LIBRARY OF CONGRESS CATALOG CARD NUMBER 87–46139
ISBN 0-06-015935-9

89 90 91 92 93 CC/HC 10 9 8 7 6 5 4 3 2 1

To my mother and father, with love

CONTENTS

ACKNOWLEDGMENTS

RECOVERING FROM A BROKEN HEART drew from the rich influence of many. Among those deserving acknowledgment are Jimi Millikan and Tom Hanna, former professors who escorted me into the exciting atmosphere of philosophical thought and never let me forget that the heart is a trusty shelter. I am obliged to Sants Kirpel and Darshan Singh for their tireless compassion and wisdom, and for teaching me much over the past two decades about patience, honesty, and letting go. Sloan Wilson, noted author, mentor, and friend, has been available as always to contribute his incomparable wit and professional guidance; his vivacious wife, Betty, gave me much support during those days when my own storm was howling. I am deeply grateful also to Charlie Beall, Cathy Turner, and Herman Levy, three teaching colleagues and comrades whose great sensitivity and courage in dealing with some of life's toughest challenges have been exemplary. Similarly, I am indebted to the Reverend Thaxton Springfield, whose credo, "People are more important than principles," has stayed with me for the many years I have worked to live up to it. Richard Stone, whose philosophical training and empathy have made him an irreplaceable ally, has shown unfailing interest in the evolution of this book and its author. My brother, Bob, con tributed his excellent thinking to help get the manuscript into final form. I also thank my sister, Linda, for her support and her invincible spirit and acknowledge friends Daniel Salvano, Henry and Connie Gooch, Norman Hering, Kären Neustadt, Brent Weinman, Tina Carlton, Bill Hutchinson, Jean Mezera, Kris and Steve Bercov, Pete Fisher, Gretchen Gross, and Saviz and Maheen Shafaie—for their skilled listening and loving presence, and for reminding me of life's goodness when I was least able to feel it. The conversations we had furthered my recovery and led to many of the understandings that appear throughout this work. I am also grateful to Denise Renton for her love, encouragement, interest, and gentle clarity.

My daughter, Sam, has been a constant source of joy and inspiration in serving as a vivid reminder of how beautiful and rewarding the cocreative venture that builds families can be. Without her patience in the face of the difficulties this project imposed on our daily schedule and her endless, effortless enthusiasm, the project could not have progressed as smoothly as it did. I am indebted, too, to my parents, for more than the obvious—of all the couples I have known, they most fully embody the love and dignity of a partnership sure enough of itself to last the brief span we call a life. Their caring and eagerness to help have been, as always, indispensable, as were several discerning manuscript notes provided by my mother. Literary colleagues Elizabeth Frost Knappman of New England Publishing Associates and Shaye Areheart gave unfailing encouragement and played key roles in moving the manuscript toward publication. I am grateful to Jeanne Flagg, who helped to establish a general course for revision work, and to my talented editor, Margaret Wimberger, for her gentleness and enthusiasm, her insightful and sensitive thinking, and her wholehearted participation in the vision behind the words. I thank the members of the publishing board at Harper & Row for believing in the manuscript enough to take it to press, as well as those artists, copy editors, and others on the staff who played a part in getting it there.

One parenthetical note on style: I have opted to avoid the

cumbersome "he or she" and "himself or herself" constructions, as I am in agreement with Fowler that the considerateness of such phrases does not justify their awkwardness in most cases. Therefore, and since this work is the account of my own, incidentally male journey, I have simply used "he" unless "he or she" clearly added to the clarity or impact of the sentence.

Now: A broken heart is not something to be kept waiting. You, dear reader, may well be in terrible emotional pain. If so, consider that the journey we are about to make together opens us up to greater life and identity than we may have imagined. Only by our willingness to make this journey of recovery can we find the joy in being alive that we may all ultimately be searching for. That joy is well described in a line of verse my daughter wrote when she was five:

> *The rain stops,*
> *the flowers come out,*
> *and I see . . .*
> *it is what I always wanted.*

Along the way of recovery, I wish you a hearty Godspeed.

PHILIP GOLABUK

PREFACE

RECOVERING FROM A BROKEN HEART was set into motion by the end of a marriage, an experience that, for reasons I am still understanding, had a profoundly transformative effect on my life and my sense of who I am. Over the three years during which the manuscript was taking shape, I must have shared with dozens of people that I was writing a book about getting over the pain of being left by a partner, and the response was invariably, "Oh, I need to read that!" This bolstered my confidence in the relevance of the project and gave me a sense that the phenomenon of "adult abandonment," as I came to think of it, was far more common than I had understood or appreciated; I began to suspect that the suffering over being left was widespread in our society. In this case, however, misery was poor company, and, even while working on the book, I felt no sense of purpose. The first draft turned out to be largely a half-inspired, half-confused outpouring of unresolved emotion. While of therapeutic value to me, it would undoubtedly have proven worthless to my reader, amounting as it did to little more than a smoke screen of rationalizations masking the sorrow and rage that had come to predominate in my heart and from which I was beginning to feel no escape was possible. Exhaustion gave way to the exhaustion beyond exhaustion. There seemed to be no hope either of reunion or recovery.

Then, somehow—perhaps it was out of sheer weariness—I began to let go, just a little, began to accept the storm that was raging within me rather than denying and running from it. This simple act of wearied acquiescence opened my heart enough for a new understanding of what I was going through to begin to emerge. I had no idea of where it would lead; the overriding emotional climate within me was still one of grief and anger but now something else had my attention. As recovery gained a solid footing, I started to see my predicament from an entirely different angle, one that was quite unexpected and, incidentally, called for considerable reworking of the manuscript. All in all, *Recovering* was rewritten four times, evolving as I evolved, deepening as the awareness of recovery deepened. The work became gentler, less bitter. Sections were amended, added, cut away—in some cases, new insights directly contradicted the ones they replaced. It was quite a ride.

I have since come to a better appreciation of the depth of the wounds so many of us have sustained and carry in our heart, and I suspect that recovery, once begun, is ongoing. Certainly, the forces of transformation that gave rise to *Recovering* continue in my life, and the story unfolds without pause. I would encourage my reader to approach this book in a spirit of receptive investigation, to take it to heart, use what is useful, and leave the rest. After all, any such work is to its author's life what a bookmark is to a book: It points, for the time being, to the place he was when he stopped writing and records, for anyone who is interested, how things have gone thus far. Any author, especially one who writes from the heart of his most personal experiences, is susceptible to holding onto his work too long: He does not want to let it go lest he learn something wonderful a day later. But there is a time to let things go. There is always more to learn, more to live, more to love. And since each life is unique, anything of value you find in these pages is best taken as a point of departure for your own continued recovery and growth.

If there were one message I could send you at this moment, it would be simply that your suffering is not pointless. Within it is the opportunity for transformation to the higher equilibrium of a new way of being. An experimental faith in the possibility of this new way of being is needed in the beginning, precisely because it *is* new, but there is little to lose in exploring the possibility when the alternative is staying stuck in heartache. Recovery will release you from the grip of confusion, fear, anger, and pain, and will usher in a natural renaissance of clarity, creativity, forgiveness, love, and self-esteem. As hard as it may be for you to believe at this time, you can recover from the great injury of a broken heart and wake up glad to be alive again. Furthermore, recovery is not far away, for the nature of the heart is wholeness, and, despite the evening news, joyful awareness, not suffering, is our birthright.

With this possibility as a beginning, perhaps we will be open to going beyond the sometimes terribly convincing feeling that life, along with our partner, has abandoned us. Such openness helps a little, and where nothing seems to help much, a little is a lot. In this spirit, all that follows is offered.

And ruined love,
when it is built anew,
Grows fairer than at first,
more strong, far greater.

—SHAKESPEARE
Sonnet 119

THE
JOURNEY BEGINS

━━━━━━━━━

*We shall find peace. We shall hear the angels, we
shall see the sky sparkling with diamonds.*

—ANTON CHEKHOV
Uncle Vanya

STORMS

Yes, it's happening to you. You've been left by the most important adult in your life and it feels awful. Suddenly, you find yourself caught in a storm of emotions that continually threatens to engulf you. Rage, fear, disbelief, hopelessness, pain, and shock have gathered within you like dangerous, dark thunderheads, unleashing their fury, it may seem, every minute of the day. And how many minutes there are in a day when you are watching the clock or waiting for the mail or a phone call! You function on "automatic." Even when you manage to become distracted at work or home, there is always the sense that something is profoundly wrong, an undertow of distress, anxiety, dislocation. What you're going through has been rated on the scale of stress-producing experiences as about the worst. The dreadful possibility you may have suspected, feared, or denied for months, perhaps years, is now a reality. Your partner is gone. *Gone.* Your life is ruined, and there is nothing you can do about it.

This feeling of hopelessness, however pervasive it may seem, is a delusion. In fact, while there may be nothing you can do to help bring about a reconciliation with your former partner, there is a great deal you can do to help heal the wounds within yourself. Despite the way you may feel right now, you can recover your vitality, you can heal, you can return to life. Furthermore, although time is a factor and the process seems to be ongoing, this journey is not a long one, for its destination, as Tennyson described in "The Higher Pantheism," is closer than breathing and nearer than our hands and feet. We can begin this curious journey by opening our awareness to three things. First:

1. *Things change.*

Change is an inexorable law of life. Things changed to this; they will change again. It is not important at this point to try to anticipate *how* they will change, but simply to recognize and appreciate as much as possible that they will. You are not condemned to suffer forever the pain of having been abandoned. The second:

2. *You will change.*

In time, with even the slightest willingness on your part, the life within you will transform you to whatever degree necessary to return you to emotional health and strength. Seeds planted beneath concrete find a way out—around and between cracks or up through the concrete itself if no easier path is allowed—and the human spirit is no less determined. At deep levels, changes are already being set into motion, changes that will restore your sense of connection with life, with or without your partner. This is automatic. We can delay the expression of the life within us, but it is nearly impossible to grieve forever. Recovery is as natural as the movement of clouds and the changing of the seasons. The third, and perhaps most important point:

3. *Feelings are not facts.*

Feeling powerless is not the same as being powerless. Feeling worthless is not the same as being worthless. Recovery depends upon our learning to accept our feelings *as feelings*, to acknowledge them with compassion, and to refrain from condemning, avoiding, or judging any of them, especially the most negative. No feeling need be taken immediately as an accurate report of your world or its possibilities. This is important because whenever we suffer rejection, emotional vampires come out in force. These are the negative thoughts and feelings that sap our strength, convince us that we cannot survive, and imbue all our flaws and mistakes, real or imagined, with depressing significance. At such times, we may respond with an almost overwhelming urge to curl up and disappear, to escape from the pain even if it means giving up our very existence.

Being rejected by the person you love will tend to trigger a painful series of secondary self-rejections until you are so caught up in the grip of all this that you can hardly distinguish original from added injury. As time passes, you may *feel* less and less whole, less and less desirable, less and less capable of that joyful, involved participation in life that is now almost beyond remembering. Nevertheless, the worst of feelings notwithstanding, you possess untapped resources that can almost immediately provide some degree of relief. For now, it is important that you at least experimentally believe there may be more you can do to promote your own healing than you *feel* you can do and that the feeling of helplessness, while understandable, is just a feeling you're having about yourself and not an accurate report of your situation.

TEN UMBRELLAS

PERHAPS THE WORST PAIN of a broken heart is that the heart is not broken entirely, once and for all, whereupon, at least, the suffering would be over, but rather it keeps breaking. The pain does not seem to pass; it plants itself in the chest, an aching disappointment that moves in and takes over like an unwanted relative, and it can stay many months, even years. Of course, profound disappointment is to be expected when someone we love and trust chooses to leave, but when it becomes chronic, when it seems to get in the way of our being fully alive, it is another matter entirely. Past a certain point it takes tremendous effort to stay in pain. The sense that one is *trapped* in the pain points to a deep resistance to the changing forces of life. We build this resistance largely by dwelling on the worst of what's happening, by getting lost in self-recrimination, by being impatient, and by confusing feelings with facts. The following ten "umbrellas" gently lessen this resistance by reminding us of what is real and by encouraging hope, patience, and kindness toward ourselves. They can do a great deal to shelter us from the rain when the emotional storms are raging.

 1. There is a difference between what I feel and what is real. I can acknowledge and accept my feelings *as feelings* without getting lost in them.

2. I am in a period of emotional shock to which I am fully entitled. Healing and feeling healthy may take some time.

3. All things considered, I did the best I could. I can learn from what I have lived through, go on, and do better. I do not have to blame myself, even if I made mistakes.

4. Negative thoughts and feelings are like the draining of an infection. I understand that any fearful, self-blaming, or destructive imagining is my mind's way of releasing the pain I am in. Therefore, I will not get negative about being negative.

5. I lived before I met my partner; I can live again.

6. I do not have to be alone. Beautiful expressions of life are available to me in various forms: family, friends, children, pets, and nature.

7. There are no unhappy endings because there are no endings.

8. Anything is possible for me.

9. I do not have to make any decisions right now.

10. The depth of all I am feeling shows me that I am an alive and caring human being. Even if my worth is not apparent to me, I will affirm it each day. I declare solidarity with myself. *I* will not leave me.

At this point, you have an emotional tightrope to walk: accepting your feelings fully, not repressing them by parading a false smile, and so on, and at the same time remembering that they are "just" feelings—feelings that are perfectly appropriate to your situation but not necessarily accurate indicators of what is real about you or possible for you. Finding this balance may take a little practice, but it will spare you the self-perpetuating emotional storms that can exhaust you and delay healing. Allow yourself to feel what you feel. If that means holding your pillow at night and crying your eyes out, go ahead. Feelings accepted *as feelings* need not intimidate. The crying, the anger, the pain—all will pass; like a pitcher, you will empty of them eventually. Acknowledging and expressing your feelings in this way is an important act of self-solidarity. It affirms the fact that you are an important, valuable person, and in so doing, promotes recovery.

Regardless of how you may be feeling, you can find many ways to affirm your own worth. Reading this book is itself such an act of affirmation. You can take walks, keep a journal, treat yourself to dinner at a favorite restaurant. Despite the present emotional constrictions of anger and pain, your life is a rich story whose unfolding is much greater than any single chapter, no matter how painful or joyous. If you find it difficult or even impossible to feel the truth of this, act as though you feel it and, before long, it will begin to prove itself in your experience. So often, we refuse to try something until we understand how and why and when it will work; we are unwilling to make the initial investment without a guarantee. This may make good sense in business, but in matters of the heart, it is the other way around: Only by first trusting a little can we begin to understand. Take a chance, therefore, on faith in your worth, even if you do not feel that this faith is warranted. Practice believing as much as possible, find little ways each day to care for yourself, and stay receptive. In time, as you heal, the unique value of who you are will become increasingly apparent to you.

Now, let's take a closer look at our ten umbrellas:

> 1. *There is a difference between what I feel and what is real. I can acknowledge and accept my feelings as feelings without getting lost in them.*

It is essential to remember this. You have already been battered around by frighteningly intense emotions that often fluctuate with distressing rapidity: grief one moment, rage the next. On Tuesday, you're seriously considering murder; on Wednesday, you're hating yourself for not having been more understanding ("If only I had . . . "). By this time, no doubt, you've taken full inventory of your many failings. Recognize that these self-judgments are a by-product of what is happening to you and, unlike legitimate insights into how you might be able to be more honest or more loving, have no bearing on who you are. Such insights arise in us when we are able to look at ourselves with kind eyes, while self-judgment is harsh and only blocks the way to deeper understanding and growth. Again, feeling worthless does not make you worthless. Feeling undesirable does not mean you are undesirable. Feeling that life simply cannot go on does not pull the sun from the sky or stop your lungs from naturally taking their next breath. In your present emotional state, however, the reassurance of "this, too, shall pass" may not have much impact. Faith is needed in the early stages—faith that pain passes, that relief comes, that nightmares end, that this nightmare will end. Gradually, naturally, relief *will* replace the pain that holds us hostage when we suffer betrayal, rejection, and abandonment, and when it does come, *relief will be just as real as pain is now.* Until it is, honor your feelings as feelings with a loving, almost protective attitude, as though your tears, gritting teeth, and wringing hands were children who need your patient attention, who need to act out their frustration so they can get it out of their system and feel calm again. This will be far easier if you keep in mind that feelings are not facts. Acknowledged, they are transitions. This is especially so in times of deep hurt.

> 2. *I am in a period of emotional shock to which I am fully entitled. Healing and feeling healthy may take some time.*

You *are* in shock. The injured "children" of your emotions *do* need your help, perhaps desperately. One of the greatest things you can contribute to your own healing is patience. You have experienced a deep wounding that must eventually transform into deep recovery, and impatience will work against you in the same way picking at a scab reopens a cut. Healing takes time, though you can find some relief fairly quickly by using the ideas presented here. Do not place much importance on self-criticism at this point, for example, "Why can't I shake this off?," "I'm leaning on my friends too much," and "My family is probably sick of hearing about this—it's been three months!" Enlist the support of those who love you by helping them to understand that your talking specifically about whatever is hurting you is a vital part of the healing process. Never mind if "it doesn't make any sense" to go over and over the same thoughts, feelings, and memories again and again. *Do this as much as you feel you need to, at this point.* Tell the story a thousand times and be patient with every telling; every feeling; every round of sleeplessness; every episode of sudden, middle-of-the-night waking; every thunderclap of rage, grief, anxiety, jealousy. Later, you will "mine" these for the hidden treasures of recovery. For now, let it all out with someone you trust. Pay attention to the feelings that come up and receive them with compassion and respect, remembering that they are not factually accurate indicators. As hard—as impossible—as it may be for you to believe at this point, *the pain will pass.*

3. *All things considered, I did the best I could. I can learn from what I have lived through, go on, and do better. I do not have to blame myself, even if I made mistakes.*

In the chaos of a shattered love, there is a natural period of fallout, a period in which many if not all of our relationships are adversely affected for a while. Relatives may make the mistake of helping you ransack the past to see what you could have done better. More commonly, they will leap at chances to blame your errant partner. This can make you uncomfortable to the extent that you love the person they're condemning. Undoubtedly, they have your best interests at heart; they do not like seeing you in pain and want you to be free of it, but they may not realize that *blame is not the way out of pain.* What they (or you) call "the past" may not even be an accurate account of your history with your absent partner, but rather a series of interpretations prejudiced by the considerable pain of the present. For now, stay with the idea that, in the strictest sense of the words, you did the best you could, and when the urge to blame comes up, acknowledge it as a feeling without indulging it. There is very little value in faultfinding, which is, after all, a kind of revenge against oneself or another. Revenge keeps us stuck. As King Arthur noted, it is "the most worthless of causes."

> *4.*) *Negative thoughts and feelings are like the draining of an infection. I understand that any fearful, self-blaming, or destructive imagining is my mind's way of releasing the pain I am in. Therefore, I will not get negative about being negative.*

In her well-known book, *Freedom from Nervous Suffering,* Dr. Claire Weeks discusses "second fear." This is the fear certain people experience when they feel themselves growing afraid. They are afraid of fear; their fear is "recursive," which is to say that when they feel fear, especially if the cause of the fear is not readily apparent, they suddenly become anxious about being afraid. Because they fear being afraid, their fear is self-perpetuating. This is an awful experience; one can hardly imagine it if one has not gone through it. The same phenomenon can occur with other emotions, both positive and negative: We can be saddened by our own grief, grow hopeless over our despair or depression, feel delighted at waking up happy. This recursive aspect of emotion follows from the fact that we are self-conscious beings. We not only have subjective experiences, but are also aware to some degree that we are having them and "resonate" in kind with what we see when looking at ourselves.

Especially when someone we love has left us, storm after storm of negativity comes up, and it is important to remember that emotions can be recursive. Only in this way does it become possible to tell the difference between the terrible pain of being left and the pain generated by the pain itself. *Distinguishing between first pain and second pain is vital because the only way to short-circuit the recursive process is to become aware that it is happening.*

We have, then, *first pain* (abandonment, rejection, loss) and *second pain* (self-condemnation, wounded pride, anger at being in this position, "if only" scenes imagined to the point of exhaustion, etc.). First pain is "original" to a situation; second pain, "added." In first pain, we are hurt; in second pain, we are hurt about being hurt. First pain is anger; second pain, the feeling of being angry about our anger.[1] As a friend put it when he was helping me through a particularly rough afternoon: "Yes, it's a tragedy—don't make it a catastrophe!" Because he offered this gently, I could hear that he was not being critical. Rather, he was saying that, in view of the sad fact of my having been hurt, I did not have to hurt myself. We hurt ourselves when we interfere with our pain, either by trying to push it away or by getting so caught up in it that we magnify it into more than it is.

We cannot deny feeling whatever is in us to feel without paying a tremendous price, for through denial we only postpone feeling it and incur the additional debt of postponement. Life has a way of keeping its books, and, sooner or later, what we deny comes chasing us. Acknowledging and expressing our pain, how-

---

[1] The concept of first pain and second pain has far-reaching implications for crisis intervention and the alleviation of human suffering in many areas, such as rape counseling, bereavement counseling, suicide prevention, codependency counseling, and counseling for the terminally ill patient and his or her family. There may be no area of emotional life where the recursive character of human consciousness does not come into play, no crisis that is not aggravated by it. The ability to distinguish between these two kinds of pain so as to interrupt the self-perpetuating process, is a *sine qua non* of healing and is not difficult. Little more is required than a moment of quiet attentiveness to what we are feeling and a willingness to be honest about self-pity, martyrdom, and other painful emotions we might not like to admit we indulge in. For more on this, see "The Habit of Suffering" (pages 65–85).

ever, is not the same as *losing* ourselves in its expression, and this is why distinguishing between first pain and second pain is so important. *First pain should be acknowledged and allowed; second pain should be acknowledged and discounted.* This is because first pain, when given loving attention, exhausts itself through natural expression, leaving us free to go on, to resume our balance; second pain, on the other hand, feeds on attention, perpetuating itself and keeping us stuck.

We can see this clearly in healthy young children before they have learned to "behave," that is, to stifle the expression of feeling in order to please their parents. When a child is physically or emotionally hurt, he cries. In a while, if the source of pain is removed and he is simply held and *not distracted or interrupted,* the crying subsides. His attention, eventually freed up by the release of emotion, naturally goes on to more interesting things. In the case of infants, this "switch" can be almost immediate: wailing one second, sobbing and sniffling the next, reaching for a toy the next. Second pain in a child, on the other hand, is quite a disturbing thing to see: He is hurt; he cries; then, when the crying has spent itself, he broods, sometimes for long while, parlaying the original distress into a full-blown drama for added attention. Such a child has already been tampered with by oppressive or otherwise violent experiences and the natural, healing process has been subverted. When we unwittingly give ourselves to second pain, we turn our own considerable energies against ourselves. To promote recovery, we must learn to "catch ourselves" when we are allowing ourselves to be drawn into second-pain thoughts and emotions such as self-blame or self-pity. We will see there is much more to the story of second pain and more we can do about it, but this must come later in our journey. For now, we can begin by acknowledging second-pain feelings *as feelings,* simply witnessing them exactly as we do with first-pain feelings, before moving on: "I'm really feeling sorry for myself now," or "What's going on in me right now is the fear that I'm completely alone," and so on. Once we begin to recognize these self-inflicted wounds for what they are, our very awareness gives us the opportunity to "change the channel" and put our attention somewhere else. This takes practice, but without our attention to feed upon, second pain passes quickly of its own accord. Again, *sitting quietly and paying attention* to the pain we are feeling, rather than trying to push it away, is the first step. This allows us to identify whether we are experiencing first or second pain. If we become aware that we are feeling first pain, we will then give ourselves fully to it, feeling it all until it naturally expends itself; if we become aware that we are feeling second pain, we will acknowledge the feeling, "change channels," and go on to something else.

For example, suppose you wake up one morning in a particularly dark mood. You feel a lot of pain and, along with it, a strong urge to take the day off from your job. Perhaps you feel drawn to a quiet walk along the beach, where the deep, ancient rhythms of the waves can exert their healing influence. The plot thickens: You're not likely to call your boss and say, "I'm in a great deal of distress, so I'm going to take the day off and walk by the ocean." You weigh the possible consequences of taking time off without a legitimate "excuse." No doubt about it, you will probably have to lie, and lying, as we are taught from our earliest years, is bad. Several "conversations" may be taking place within you. Judgment: "I should go to work; lying is wrong." Fear: "I can't let myself go like this. If I stop working, I'll really fall apart!" Guilt: "Who am I to take off just because I feel like it? They need me at the office." Exhaustion, confusion: "I can't make it through another Monday—but I have to!" And so on. The question of what to do becomes pressing.

Now, let's consider that the answer really hinges on a prior question: Is the pain that the day off is intended to ease first or second pain? What, *precisely,* is hurting you? Are you feeling the weight of the broken dream or a barrage of judgments that say the breaking of the dream was your fault? One thing that will help you distinguish them is how you feel when you *pretend* the pain is not there. You can do this, for example, by as simple an act as holding your head up high and saying to yourself something like, "This is *not* going to get the better of me!" If the pain you have become aware of is first pain, this will feel like a lie. If it is second pain, however, you will feel encouraged, perhaps even a little valiant. Another, subtler way to distinguish first from second pain is to see how you feel when you let go and "give in" to the pain. *Giving in to first pain produces a sense of "taking care of business" and usually brings an immediate emotional release. Giving in to second pain feels self-indulgent and wasteful; you will sense that you are "spinning your wheels."* Finally, expressing first pain brings a return to emotional equilibrium and a greater sense of aliveness, while second pain prompts feelings of despair and hopelessness. When we express the hurt resulting from a real injury, we release our pain naturally and may even become aware while releasing it that we are being restored to our emotional center, to a place of balance and a sense of well-being. When we give in to second pain, however, we are caught in a self-perpetuating spiral of negativity within which there is no release, no constructive direction. This is why giving in to second pain produces feelings of despair and hopelessness.

Note that the word "emotion" has the same root as the word "motion." Feelings naturally move, and their movement is as essential to our integrity and health as the circulation of our blood. Giving ourselves to first pain contributes to the natural flow of emotion, while giving in to second pain impedes this flow by keeping us stuck in a self-perpetuating negativity.

Returning to the question of whether or not to take the day off: If you determine that you are in fact feeling first pain, call your office, tell your white lie, and go to the beach, knowing that taking care of yourself is a "higher" truth than mechanically living up to some principle of never stating something that is not literally the case. Walking beside the waves, you will find comfort in knowing that such a courageous act—and this is what it is—rightly acknowledges that your recovery is more important than Monday's agenda. If, on the other hand, you determine that you are feeling second pain, refuse to indulge in it. Instead, acknowledge it and go to work. Remember: Giving in to first pain is an act of self-care that will empower you—you will *feel* stronger;

giving in to second pain is an act of self-indulgence that will keep
you feeling stuck.

In all cases, calm yourself, take slow, deep breaths into your
lungs, and pay attention to your own heart, by which I mean
quite literally the area of feeling in the center of your chest. First
pain, when unimpeded, wells up spontaneously and with a certain conviction. One does not have to "get into" the role. Acknowledge this pain, accept it, let it come, let the storm do its
worst. Seek outside support from family and friends, lick your
wounds—but do not allow yourself to inflict new wounds in
order to lick them. By following this simple process of quieting
yourself, identifying first or second pain, and responding as indi-
cated, you will find you can become aware of the natural motion
of your own feelings and navigate through whatever pain comes
up, no matter how great. ✓

5. *I lived before I met my partner; I can live again.*

This idea is difficult in the beginning. Take it as an exercise, especially if your heart was broken recently. Simply recall
as many good things as you can about how your life was before
you met your now-absent partner. Have you taken any time to
consider it? You accomplished things, enjoyed happy moments,
laughed at jokes. Perhaps you spent more time with friends than
you may have in a while, had fewer responsibilities, were more
footloose. You might have had a special place that was yours
alone—by a lake, the beach, the woods, a certain street you liked
to bike or walk along. Did you write your innermost thoughts
and feelings in a journal or find a creative outlet in painting,
singing, or sewing? Maybe you took dance classes and felt a
greater sense of connection with your body. The point is not to
focus on "I can live without my partner" in some tense, stoic
manner. Rather, allow yourself to remember something of the
goodness of your own identity, your own self that has always
been with you.

One of the most wonderful things about being in love is that it seems to bring out our best self. The beloved holds up a mirror of affection and esteem in which we can perceive ourselves as charming, desirable, talented, witty, and in many ways uniquely valuable. It is painful when this mirror is taken away and we can no longer see ourselves so beautifully reflected, but taking away the mirror and therefore the reflection does not take away the qualities. We still possess our best qualities; we are still worthy of love. As we gradually give this wonderful self that we are more and more attention, we find ourselves increasingly able to *feel* our own strength, talent, and worth. *Recognize that the wonderful self you are has never abandoned you and never will.* It has greater vitality than you may have imagined. Open yourself to feeling its presence within you; it is your greatest ally. It will strengthen and heal you, if only you will begin to recognize and believe in it.

As an extension of this exercise, you may want to try recalling some of the tangible difficulties of life with your former partner. This should not be taken as a suggestion to plunder the past for painful memories. It is natural to romanticize the past, especially if the present is extremely painful, but doing so involves us in a kind of dishonesty that only compounds our suffering. Perhaps there were chronic fights, tensions, worries, or worse. At least *that* is over, too. Now, we can take a deep breath and rest for a while in the appreciation that these destructive forces are gone.

 6. *I do not have to be alone. Beautiful expressions of life are available to me in various forms: family, friends, children, pets, and nature.*

The feeling of isolation at a time like this can be formidable. Consequently, one of the best things you can do is surround yourself with life—with friends and relatives who care and can support you on your terms. This may largely involve their listening without judging either you or your former partner. It is hard to imagine a greater compassion than this sort of attentive, heartfelt listening; a tender hand can bring about more healing than the most astute reasoning. Beyond friends and relatives, life *is* within and all around you, even if you can't feel it or connect with it for now. If birds sing outside your window in the morning, listen to them. Pretend they are singing for *you*. One woman who wrestled for months with severe depression after being abandoned by her husband of fifteen years was suddenly uplifted when she noticed a mockingbird rubbing its beak against the bark of a tree, singing for all it was worth. Such spontaneous moments of recovery are beyond logic. They are nonetheless real.

You need not date or otherwise force yourself into social situations you don't feel ready to handle, but it is essential that you reach out as well as in. A hug from a friend, a pair of understanding eyes, the responsive purr of a trusting cat—these convey love and exert a healing influence. Make yourself available to them as much as you can. The pain may be there, even while you are reaching out to caring others. Let that be for now. One day the very real pain of the present will seem like a dream from which you awoke a long time ago.

7. *There are no unhappy endings because there are no endings.*

We may believe we have lost the dearest love we will ever know, that we will never meet anyone as wonderful as the person who has gone, and that, in this sense, love has ended for us. It serves us well to remember at such a time that things change and that there is a great deal beyond what we see contributing to the outcome of any difficulty. Much suffering comes from self-inflicted imaginings and impatience (second pain). There is a lot to be said for stepping back from a compromised situation once you have done your best to influence it and turning the matter over to whatever "bigger hands" you believe there may be. We can't see how things will turn out. I know of one couple who divorced after nine years of marriage. Each remarried. Then, seven years later, after divorcing their respective second spouses, they met again, worked through the deep hurts they had inflicted on themselves and each other, and, with a renewed sense of love, clarity, and commitment, remarried. In another case, the separation before remarriage lasted over twenty years! While these are extraordinary examples, they illustrate the point that life is fundamentally mysterious and unpredictable. Only our arbitrary assigning of conclusions gives the impression that there are "dead ends." It is possible that years from now, when you are well beyond the pain that now seems so unrelenting, the bond you cocreated with your partner may again beckon, suddenly, unplanned, like the rose thrown unexpectedly into a room through an open window, described by Hāfez, the Persian mystic poet. Or, it may go differently: Another gifted poet from the East, Rabindranath Tagore, writes of losing his beloved and vowing never to love again, until one day he catches the gaze of a pair of brown eyes across the room and everything changes. Possibility, surprise, the unexpected—these are inherent in the unfolding of events if we are willing to see them. We do not know what life will bring us tomorrow.

Indeed, being left by someone we love forces us to feel the hardest edge of that uncertainty and subjects the mind to an avalanche of painful questions. How has this happened? Where will it lead? Can I trust again? Is reconciliation possible? Within all this uncertainty, one thing is certain: *You can go on with your life.* This is the direction for now. Later, if the possibility of reconciliation presents itself, there will be many issues to address that simply cannot be productively addressed at this time—issues of forgiveness, rebuilding trust, establishing limits and conditions, avoiding old habits of poor communication. Or, like Tagore, you may, without expecting to, find yourself opening up to the possibility of a richer bond with someone else. In any case, trying to resolve these matters now is fruitless and depleting, precisely because they are matters for two to work out, not one. Whether you eventually reconcile with your partner or not, the present situation will change in time.

8. *Anything is possible for me.*

This will probably feel like an outright lie. It is hard to believe in the future when it takes all your strength just to get up, get dressed, and concentrate on the simplest task at hand. Nevertheless, the only thing keeping you from feeling the truth of this is the emotional storm you are going through. Remember, feeling is not fact. You are free to affirm this truth, that anything is possible for you, despite the fact that you may not be able to feel its truth for now. *The feeling that nothing is possible ("all is lost") is second pain.* Life is rich in possibility; you may not be able to see the truth of this now, but you will see it before long if you are even the least bit willing to lift your eyes from the ground. As your psyche releases its pent-up emotions and your focus of attention shifts from injury to recovery, you will awaken to possibility, feel it again in your life. There is no shortcut. Until the release of these emotions is well along, you will feel as though all possibility for happiness left with your partner. Again, recognize this as a natural feeling that is emotionally valid but factually inaccurate. *Possibility opens up in our lives as we are able to make ourselves receptive to it.* We cannot have what we are not open to having, a principle implicit in such spiritual sayings as "Ask and you shall receive." Openness to possibility is the beginning of experience in the world. Therefore, regardless of how you feel, remind yourself each day that anything is possible for you. This includes the possibilities of recovery, reconciliation, new partnership, and joyful, nonpartnership living.

9. *I do not have to make any decisions right now.*

Let things be for a while, even if they don't make any sense. Let them be crazy. Take time, as much as you want. If you're in doubt about a certain course of action, hold off for now. Should I call? Not call? Write? Start going out with someone else? Trust again? These will all fall into place in time, so there is no need to force anything. You have only one direction to follow: Let yourself heal, with support from caring others. The decisions can wait for another day.

10. *The depth of all I am feeling shows me that I am an alive and caring human being. Even if my worth is not apparent to me, I will affirm it each day. I declare solidarity with myself. I will not leave me.*

We have all had experiences that hurt us, that made us feel inadequate and unworthy. As children, even our natural impulses led to censure as we became socialized. We learned early that we had to live up to the expectations of those on whom we depended for love. Many times, this love was withheld or even taken away, leaving us feeling guilty, unworthy, rejected. We quickly learned to be "good," to earn love, and in the process we lost touch with the one person whose love for us matters most: ourselves. During my years as a college teacher, I was continually astonished at how difficult it was for students to accept praise, especially in front of others. Even in cases where that praise was clearly well deserved, they looked down at the ground, made excuses, became visibly uncomfortable. The few students who could muster a "thank you" seemed to choke on the words. They simply could not bring themselves to emotionally "own" what was talented, beautiful, or brilliant about themselves. Far more than mere self-consciousness in front of the group, this was clearly a deep-seated *inability to see* that they did, in fact, possess outstanding, laudable qualities. In most cases, this difficulty seemed to stem from a conviction, largely unexamined, that it is wrong to appreciate oneself, that there is something arrogant about doing so. Many of us have been taught that it is bad to celebrate our own goodness; that we should look outside ourselves for love, approval, and appreciation; and—here is the most astonishing part—that upon receiving these, we must reject them straightaway! By the time we are adults, this self-rejection is quite practiced, and we may feel the self cannot be trusted. We may even believe, as many seem to, that the self is a repository of repressed and dark urges that, if unchecked by conscience, will unleash violence in all directions.

Now, multiply such a self-deprecating belief by the emotional force of abandonment, and the likely result is a person struggling fiercely against a profound feeling of unworthiness. Here is where we can make good use of the idea that feelings are not facts. As we proceed along the path of recovery, we will see that our own knee-jerk reactions to our feelings have helped create many of the painful situations we then came to believe had been inflicted on us. It is possible to acknowledge feelings and *respond* rather than react to them. It is possible to watch a strong feeling come, peak, diminish in intensity, and, finally, go. As we practice paying attention to our feelings as feelings, we begin to realize that *we can experience even our strong emotions without jumping in and losing ourselves in them.* I was amazed the first time I was able to do this with anger, an emotion I have always experienced as a particularly powerful "siren song." It is tremendously liberating to realize that we can feel such an emotion and not identify with it. Here, we have a foundational principle of recovery:

> *Suffering arises out of the identification of the self with painful emotions, thoughts, and sensations.*

To compassionately watch our emotions and attendant bodily sensations—tightness in the chest, "electricity" in the hands, a "lump in the throat," and so on—noting them without judgment of any kind, is much easier than it sounds if we follow this simple procedure:

> *Stop, pay attention from the heart. Compassionately note whatever feelings present themselves. Watch them come. Watch them go. Let them go.*

Take time with each step. The effect is a little like the old trick of counting to ten when one is in danger of losing his temper. *Stopping* interrupts the momentum of habit long enough for us to *pay attention from the heart* and become aware of what is going on within us. It is essential to do this *from the heart:* This is not an exercise in disembodied, analytical self-watching, but a movement toward the open heart that can actually be felt in the chest area. Only from the heart is it possible *to compassionately note* what we are feeling, including both emotions and physical sensations, and to gently acknowledge and affirm them without either judging or identifying with them. The shift from unconscious identification to wholehearted witnessing gives us the distance we need to avoid becoming caught up in what we are feeling. All feelings pass; they are under the jurisdiction of the law of change—in fact, they change from moment to moment and are only given longevity by our identifying with them. As we watch a feeling change, and especially as its intensity begins to diminish, we can help it pass by simply cooperating with this natural process, by not holding on, by *letting go.* Then, in the clarity and openness of this broadened awareness arising in the heart, we can choose what is really important to us in the situation and respond accordingly through action. Recovery, more than anything else, is this process of unconditional self-compassion that allows us to become aware of our feelings as feelings, and to choose whether or not to give ourselves to them. By becoming aware in this way, we can replace knee-jerk reactions to our own feelings with heartfelt responses that put us in touch with the tremendous life within us. We can thus appreciate and express the natural joy of our innate worth, *no matter what we are feeling in a given moment.*

Developing this awareness is simply a matter of paying attention. When we get caught up in something, we usually ignore a great deal going on right around it. We become highly selective, ignoring whatever lies outside our immediate purpose. "When a pickpocket meets a saint," the saying goes, "all he sees are his pockets." In the same way, we are so accustomed to identifying ourselves with the "noise" of our thoughts and feelings that it hardly ever occurs to us to simply pay attention to it without jumping into the fracas, to watch the traffic go by without catching a ride, as my friend Norman put it once. When anger comes, we identify with it and react: "*I* am angry." When sexual desire comes, we react: "*I* am turned on." When fear comes, we react: "*I* am afraid." The identification of the self with the feeling is instantly there. We seldom take a calm stand in simple awareness. We are "taken in" by our emotions and identify with them with the speed of a habit reinforced countless times. Until we begin to pay careful attention to whatever is going on in and around us, exactly as it is, letting our feelings come and go with a loving detachment, we cannot begin to wake up to our heart. We will continue to react and react from within the constrictions of our own willfulness. And we will continue to suffer.

Practicing awareness means watching sadness, for example, without *becoming* sad. It means watching it until it passes in order to understand something about the nature of this strong emotional state, in order to begin to see that we are not that emotion. The sadness is noted, simply that, with an attentive, nonjudging, nonidentifying awareness. "Sadness is here," not "I am sad." Gradually, it becomes clear: We *experience* that we are something greater than anything we may be experiencing. We are the *experiencer*. We do not *have* to identify with the endless coming and going, the relentless turmoil. We do not have to cling to any of it. We have a choice. And having a choice means we do not have to suffer.

NOW THAT YOU'RE ALONE, YOU'RE NOT ALONE

ONE OF THE PARADOXES of human life is that, though each of us is a sovereign being with a unique point of view and subjective "territory," we are never really alone, and while it is fashionable to believe we are "born alone and die alone," this hardly seems to be so. No one is born without a mother. We are in the company of others during our early years; later, we discover teachers and friends at school; as adults, we are given opportunities for greater intimacy. The mind itself, with which we usually identify, comprises a self that talks to us in our head and a self that listens and responds in a perpetual dialogue. In this sense, the mind is a roommate of sorts to whom we "come home" when we introspect. Perhaps even death, which often comes as a friend to those ready for it, escorts us beyond the confines of earthly experience into vaster realms of relation. Although we may feel utterly alone, we are never entirely forsaken.

As you move through the transition from suffering to recovery, you can draw from many sources to assuage your loneliness. Life has given you caring friends and family, as well as guidance in the form of books, tapes, and other resources to help you through the shock of having been left. Open yourself to them. Do not, in reaching toward a deeper and clearer awareness of your identity, cut yourself off from those valuable mirrors that can hold up to you images of your own innate goodness, strength, and worth. Remember: *It is most important that the practice of inner awareness—stopping, paying attention, noting our feelings, and so on— be based on compassion.* We do not watch ourselves with the mind, but with the heart. And we know the difference. *When we are in our mind, the most we end up with is being right. When we are in our heart, we end up home.* Cultivate this self-compassion, which is crucial to recovery, by connecting with those who believe in and love you. Trust the simple desire for a hand, a shoulder, a kind word, a smile, some time to be heard. Reach out as a child would.

THE LAW OF OPPOSITES

As we take a little time each day to practice noting our feelings as feelings, lovingly paying attention to the ongoing stream of both inner and outer experience rather than reacting mechanically out of habit, we begin to understand that the world within and around us is not a blur of blind forces, but a system following inexorable laws of polarity, reverse, and balance. The ancient Chinese text, the *Tao-te Ching*, offers penetrating insights into these laws, one of which it identifies as the "Law of Opposites." According to the book's remarkable author, Lao-tzu, who walked the sands of China five hundred years before Christ was born, everything is subject to this law. That is, everything begins, grows to a point of maturation or fullness, and then declines. As soon as anything reaches an extreme degree of any kind, its reversal is assured. "High winds don't last all morning, heavy rains don't last all day," Lao-tzu instructs. Like the ocean tide, human experiences ebb and flow in their own, natural course. If this were not true, the worst of our emotions would be a permanent prison, and no amount of awareness would liberate us from suffering.

The Law of Opposites tells us that when we try to force any situation, we only create contrary results. It is as though we are moving continuously through a revolving door; the more we push in a given direction, the faster we wind up going in the opposite one. Have you ever tried to remember the name of a television or screen actor and found that the harder you tried, the more elusive it became? Letting go of the effort to remember often allows the missing name to come to mind within a few minutes, as though of its own accord. This is the "effortless effort" (also described by Lao-tzu in the *Tao-te Ching*) in which we release ourselves from habitual patterns of thinking and relax in order to be open to receiving something rather than struggling to get it through a direct effort of will.

To illustrate: Think of someone you know who doesn't listen well, who is usually so busy talking about himself that he has no interest at all in what you have to say. Doesn't this one-sided demand for your attention make you reluctant to give it? On the other hand, someone who can listen well earns a willing audience. By pushing, insisting, forcing, we create the opposite of what we want; by letting go, opening ourselves, being patient, we invite the world to come to us. "Nature abhors a vacuum," wrote the philosopher Spinoza, observing the Law of Opposites at work in the physical universe. The world balances extremes. Every increase involves a decrease. You cannot find a ten-dollar bill that someone else did not lose. There are many other examples:

> Humility invites praise.
> Bragging invites censure.
> Effort leads to rest.
> Pleasure and pain (extremes) pass.
> Criminal acts invite justice.
> One who serves others is served.
> One who will not compromise loses ground.
> One who makes allowances is forgiven.
> One who forces is pushed away.
> One who cannot be quiet will not be heard.

Understanding the Law of Opposites, one can see, appreciate, and cooperate with the fact of continual, oppositional change, both within and without. There is a saying that the Chinese know what to do when it rains: Let it rain. This is very different from the traditional Western view that seeks to control and manipulate both inner and outer nature.

As you sit quietly in your heart, paying careful attention to your feelings, you will witness many extremes. Recognize that these will pass naturally. *They will pass more readily if you don't resist them.* Resistance lends strength to the force it would oppose. It is not easy, when we are being tossed about on the stormy seas of a broken heart, to refrain from resisting the fear and pain, but resistance at such a time is misguided effort and only works against us. Even after we have tried in vain to do everything humanly possible to resolve the situation, we may feel we will go mad if we don't do *something!* The Law of Opposites encourages us to recognize that, since events are always in a process of evolution, there is nothing we need to do. Accepting this is difficult, especially when we are identified with the stream of our thoughts and feelings, the "I" that seems unceasingly bent on controlling, reacting, and doing.

We may take encouragement, then, from the fact that things return to a state of balance when left to follow their course, that they fall into place, and that this process is helped when we pay kind attention to our emotions rather than fighting or identifying with them. Within great sadness, then, given the natural unfolding of things, great release bides its time, waiting for the shift in awareness that will bring it forth. Paradoxically, the anguish we feel over a lost love can be a measure of the joy that will accompany love's resurrection, as Shakespeare so beautifully expressed in one of his sonnets: "And ruined love, / when it is built anew, / Grows fairer than at first, / more strong, far greater," whether with your former partner, with someone else, or simply with life itself. Suffering is, in this light, an extraordinary opportunity for self-healing and new-found serenity. As Marcel Proust said in his great work, *Remembrance of Things Past*, "We are healed of a suffering only by experiencing it to the full."

Here is an exercise you can do to break out of habitual reactions and to consciously and creatively use the Law of Opposites to respond to old problems in new ways: The next time you feel a strong urge to react to something in a certain way, stop, shift your awareness to the heart, acknowledge the feeling as a feeling, take a deep breath, and respond in the *opposite* way. Suppose, for example, that you are at work and your boss asks you for something in an arrogant or brusque manner—say, to get him a certain report. The urge to react by taking offense will be fairly instantaneous, so you will have to stop and take a breath if you intend to follow through on the exercise. As the feeling of offense comes, don't push it away. Note it, then take another, slow breath. What would the "opposite" response be? You might smile at your boss and say, "Is there anything else you need while I'm downstairs?" Get into the play of it, and keep in mind that you must be sincere or the whole effort will probably backfire. You will be able to be sincere if you follow the steps given. Stop, shift to the heart, note the feeling, let it come and go. You *can* choose a different response than the obvious one. It isn't so important to be offended! Do it and watch what happens. In a world where egotism and hasty identification of the self with all sorts of emotional states are the rule, a mindful, aware response is quite unexpected. If you keep true to your purpose and refrain from jumping into the emotional currents racing through you, mindfully noting them without identifying with them, you are likely, before long, to see a response in those around you, a response opposite to the usual one. By staying clear of your own storms, you hold up a living example that makes it easier for them to stay clear of theirs. In such a climate of encouragement, they are likely to come around. When we take offense, after all, we only provoke defensiveness in others. When we respond by refusing to take offense, however, we encourage them to follow our lead. The escalation of tension and antagonism is short-circuited, not by our changing anyone else, but by our changing ourselves. We should keep this in mind. Our purpose here is not to rehabilitate others, but to experience our own ability, in the heat of the moment, to become aware of our emotions, acknowledge them, watch them come and go, and choose a different response. As much as possible, keep choosing to respond rather than merely react. Breathe and watch; something new will become possible. And if you should get drawn into identifying with the hostility of the situation, return to the heart and be compassionate about that. Don't get hostile about being hostile.

You can apply this principle to feelings that come up about the love you have lost. For example, the urge to get in touch with your former partner can be upon you instantly and, it may seem, irresistibly. You may find yourself struggling over the question of whether or not to phone, remembering times you phoned and wished you hadn't, or times you didn't and later wished you had. This ambiguity is inherent in the desiring mind, which is never satisfied (something we will examine more closely later). If you find yourself in this dilemma, try this: Take a deep breath and simply notice the confusion, the indecision, the rationalizing, the way one course of action seems preferable now, the opposite a moment later. As you gently release your breath, release the struggle as well. What you are feeling is intense, but it is not you. You *can* let it go. Calmly notice the futility of this urgent, inner deadlock, then take another deep breath and move in the opposite direction: Shift to the heart, acknowledge the conflict with compassion, watch it wax and wane as all conflicts do if left to run their course, and, when you are ready, move on by giving your attention to something new. Unlike a rigid decision not to call, this shift involves the ability to let go and change the channel of awareness. It can be especially powerful if (despite whatever emotional impasse there may be) you and your former partner are still seeing each other and are both at least somewhat open to the possibility of working things out together. Trying to force a reunion (through guilt, coercion, emotional bribery, pleading, reasonable arguments, threats, and other control tactics) is unlikely to produce the desired results. Moving in the opposite direction and coming from the heart with a genuine receptivity, on the other hand, can dramatically alter the terms of the encounter, making it possible for real change to occur. It is important to note that one cannot use this as a strategy for manipulating another. The Law of Opposites is inexorable, and no amount of cleverness, however sincerely motivated, can exempt us from it.

Remember that our awareness is recursive: Feelings, both positive and negative, tend to amplify themselves through the attention we give them. Granted, we may have little control over what we are feeling at a given time, but we have a great deal to say about how we *respond* to what we are feeling, and we can hurt or help ourselves by where we place our attention, by what we make important. In the example given above, we can focus on our pain, indecision, and frustration. We can continue to engage in mortal combat with life for not fulfilling our heart's desire and, in this rigid and distressed state (whether we make the phone call or not), are likely to end up not only gnashing our teeth, but gnashing our teeth over the fact that we are (once again!) gnashing our teeth—a recursive tailspin, to be sure. Or, we can change the channel, walk away from the emotional deadlock, and open ourselves to expressing life in a way life can support at this time, in which case we will end up revitalized by our own vitality—a recursive uplift. As we practice relaxing and opening our awareness with compassion for our predicament, we find we can use this recursiveness as a rope to pull ourselves, not down into the depths of suffering, but up and out. We are free to create a heaven or a hell. This much is up to us.

More than anything else, remember to be kind to yourself. Do not get angry with yourself for being angry, or judge yourself for reacting to events. In the moment of becoming aware that you have forgotten your purpose, when you realize that you are again identifying with the suffering self, shift to the heart and pay attention. This simple practice of awareness interrupts the recursive irritations the mind seems so good at inflicting on us, especially when we are feeling low. *I cannot end anger by getting angry at it, but only by extending compassion.* I cannot ease a feeling of having been betrayed by betraying myself with some self-imposed obligation to be forgiving. I can only ease the terrible constriction of such a feeling by creating an emotional and spiritual roominess within which the feeling itself is forgiven, accepted, and allowed to pass naturally. Moving in the opposite direction is a wonderful, sometimes saving technique, especially for those who feel a calling to any sort of spiritual growth. *By paying kind attention to the constriction of our suffering, we find we have the room to move beyond it.*

When I was teaching philosophy to inmates at a Florida jail, I met a prisoner who had a tremendous amount of dignity. His sense of himself was not only uninjured by the fear and cruelty inherent in the penal system, but it actually seemed to thrive under those adverse conditions. He was a young, muscular man, around twenty-five at the time; I will call him B. K. He did not say much during our classes, but he always wore a subtle smile of appreciation and listened with complete attentiveness. After several months in the jail, he was released to the custody of a halfway house. One night, standing outside, looking at the beautiful Florida night sky, he was approached by a guard who ordered him to put out his cigarette. B. K. looked at the man, dropped his cigarette, and extinguished it under his heel. The guard told him to go inside; B. K. turned to oblige.

"Wait a minute," the guard said, seeing that he was unable to provoke B. K., "I can put you on restriction any time I want."

Continuing to gaze into the sky, B. K. replied, "Look at that star, man."

"I said I can put you on restriction. I could do it right now," the guard threatened.

"Yeah, but look; it's one hell of a star," B. K. said.

Frustrated, the guard finally snarled, "Okay, that's it. You're on restriction!"

"A beautiful star," B. K. said.

At that point, the guard, incensed, said incredulously, "Didn't you hear me? I said you're on restriction! What's a damned star going to do for you now?"

B. K. turned to the guard. He was not angry. He said, simply, "I grow strong off of people like you."

Because he did not resist, because he refused the guard's invitation to do battle, he had not gotten involved in words or actions that would have made his being put on restriction appear justified. The guard was left to support the entire, oppressive effort on his own; consequently, B. K. was not put on restriction. Even if he had lost his privileges, he would not have lost what was essential to him—his freedom, which lay in his ability to respond on his own terms rather than react to another's. "The superior man cannot be beaten," Lao-tzu states, "because he does not contend."

A few months later, when he had been released from the halfway house, I ran into B. K. and he told me the story. "Let me ask you," he said. "Which one of us do you think was really locked up?"

THE MIRACULOUS SELF

WE HAVE BEEN speaking about affirming the self, about experiencing the self apart from the tangle of various thoughts, feelings, and reactions that pass through it. We have talked about the self as having the ability to refrain from identifying with these thoughts, feelings, and reactions simply by noting them with compassion. Again, the home base from which we do this noting is the heart. We note what is going on with kindness, forgiveness, and love for the self we see caught in the predicament of suffering. Here, we may run into a problem similar to the one many of my students had, that is, hearing the term "self-love" as "selfishness." Having suffered early hurts and disappointments, perhaps even having seen one or both parents model submissiveness and self-denial as humility, many of us experience self-appreciation as arrogance, and we are loath to explore celebrating our own worth. A number of recent books advise us of the importance of self-esteem but provide no real understanding of how to cultivate it when the poor self we are supposed to be holding in such esteem is steeped in negativity and feelings of worthlessness. What can "self-love" mean to a person who feels miserable about his life? The issues have become confusing, and it takes a steadfast inner listening and uncompromising honesty to return to the simple experience of the self's inherent worth. Nevertheless, self-love, in the sense of unconditional self-acceptance and compassion for oneself, is the cornerstone of recovery.

Often, because we have such a hard time believing that we are valuable and lovable right now, exactly as we are, we must bolster our sense of self-worth by assuming that we will be lovable later, when we are older, more experienced, smarter, more mature, better looking, kinder, more creative, financially better off, and so on. To be sure, ideals can stir us to develop our character, to patiently and courageously practice our dreams and thereby make them gradually more real in our life, but only if we begin from where we are now, in a spirit of self-acceptance and cooperation. Without this willingness to accept ourselves as we are, we sentence ourselves to anger, conflict, confusion, resentment, guilt, blame, and fear. In an emotional climate of negativity and resistance, inner growth is impossible. Real and lasting movement toward any goal or ideal always begins here and now with an act of acceptance. We build who we can be on the solid foundation of a loving regard for who we are. Honesty and compassion form this foundation, not a judgmental attitude that is forever postponing our worth in our own eyes. "Better is the enemy of good," the expression warns. Loving who we can be does not require that we condemn or deny who we are, any more than loving ourselves as we are has to diminish our desire to become more.

WHO DO YOU THINK YOU ARE?

To some degree, we experience the loss of a loved one as a loss of who we are because our identity is deeply bound up with those we love. We are mother, father, daughter, son, wife, husband, sister, brother, friend—all these important relationships give us a sense of ourselves; losing one or more of them robs us of deeply familiar ways of being in our world and belonging to it. We may not realize that we have so identified ourselves with these relationships that we no longer experience ourselves as existing in our own right, as it were, apart from them. Being on the road to recovery means that we are committed to rediscovering the identity that is always ours no matter how much we may invest it in relationships. To do this, we must begin to distill our "original" self out from the many things with which it has identified, the many things it has come to believe are itself. This original self is like a silk tossed over the cactus of the world. Caught on its many needles, it has taken on the shape of the prickly plant and no longer expresses its light, flowing nature. To free it without tearing, we must proceed slowly, lifting it gently off one thorn at a time. There is no need to rush. We are simply going to ask who we think we really are.

Consider: If asked who you are, you would not answer, "I am my car, my house, my clothes," and so on. You would not confuse yourself with the things you own, your property, the many things you describe by using this word, "my." Now, the first thing we see when we look for the self is that it cannot be found and that, when we try to articulate who we are, we end up talking in the language of ownership. Thus, we say *my* name, *my* history, *my* body, *my* feelings, *my* soul. Note, however, that, just as in the case of material property, none of this "stuff" is ever what we really mean by "I" and that whatever is doing all this owning seems to refuse to make itself apparent. The self "hides" from itself then, behind the language of its "property," never standing forth and showing itself as itself, apart from all it owns. How strange that, despite our taking the self utterly for granted, what we are, as the *experiencer,* is elusive, even baffling. Quite literally, we have no *idea* of who we are. We seem to be a total mystery to ourselves. What are we to do with this mystery?

Let us examine the matter more closely. When you say "I," what do you mean? We all use this unobtrusive little word countless times each day, but are we ever clear about what it refers to? The word "apple" is not the apple itself; the word "fire" does not burn. Similarly, the word "I" is not the self it seems to name. Do we have any idea what this self is? Whatever this "I" is, this personal center of identity, it is not a fixed thing; it can *shift*. We experience this shift in the practice of noting feelings from the heart rather than reactively judging them or identifying with them. As we go deeper into heart-awareness, we may be startled by the changes we feel ourselves undergoing. I remember my astonishment when I realized that by "I" I had always meant my *mind*, the talking voice in my head associated with rational thinking and the conscious, egocentric will. This was the part of my consciousness with which I had unknowingly identified, the part I experienced as "myself." From within that overly limiting identification, anything my mind could not grasp I experienced as "*I* don't get it." I only "got" those things I could demonstrate through argument and my well-practiced talent for being right. What presented itself to me as true, then, did so strictly in terms of the sort of adversarial, defensive thinking the mind is so good at, while the far richer truth of community and closeness remained, for the most part, foreign to my experience. As my awareness opened, however, I came to realize that this arguing voice in my head was not me, but only what I had come to believe was myself—a fearful and constricted identity isolated by its own willfulness, cut off from the immediate richness and preciousness of so much going on in and around me. Looking back, I saw that in my heart (that awareness emanating from the chest area and characterized by balance, simplicity, compassion, and gratitude), I had always known many things that I didn't realize I knew, and that it was only my mind that had not known. This is a humdinger of a paradox: The mind, which insists on knowing, churns in perpetual confusion and ambiguity and ultimately knows nothing, while the heart, which does not need to know and is at home in what Shunryu Suzuki called "beginner's mind," is peacefully clear to itself and others and, in this sense, knows all we need to know in a given situation. The mind's endless questions are answered by the heart's wisdom. I had been unable to see this because I had been involved in a lifelong case of mistaken identity.

We have all heard the teaching, "Love thyself," but this is

puzzling because how we hear this depends on what we are identified with. If we are identified with the mind, as I was, it will seem that it is the mind-self (the willful "I am" that talks to us in our head) that we are supposed to love. If we are identified with our physical attributes, self-love will evoke a sense of appreciation for how we look or perform physically. As we become more situated in the heart we find that the very suggestion to love the self elicits a fuller sense of self-affirmation and regard; in fact, to be in our heart is to already love the self. In terms of recovery, self-love does not mean self-applause or conceit. *The self-love central to recovery is nothing more than the compassionate openness that does not resist whatever is presenting itself.* It is a complete, quiet acceptance of all we are, in this moment, as it appears, right now.

We cannot *know* who we are, for knowing is a clever part of us that, somewhere along the line, got us to believe in its authority, even over areas of our experience that, strictly speaking, have nothing to do with knowing. What the mind calls "the self" and thinks it knows is not the self. Although recovery must seem elusive as long as we identify with this mind, it occurs spontaneously when we allow a shift from mind-identification and willfulness to the courageous, compassionate awareness that arises in the heart as we calmly and lovingly regard ourselves and our predicament. Who we really are is only a mystery to the mind, while the heart experiences the true self as openness, joy, balance, clarity, love, and homecoming. In this shift from head to heart, what was mysterious stands forth as miraculous, full of wonder and wonderfully familiar, and our suffering is transformed into an awakening, an opening to life beyond the forces that bring suffering into being and sustain it.

Having been abandoned by your partner, you have been thrown back on your alone-self and may have many painful moments in which you actually have no clear sense of who you are. This is natural. Memories of partnership may emphasize your aloneness by contrast, making it all the more conspicuous and painful. You may even come to experience yourself essentially in terms of the present lack. So much of life, for good or ill, was *in terms of* the bond that is now gone, and the world can seem a great, empty place when that reflection, that echo, that point of reference is no more. Our very identity seems to have vanished in the overwhelming emptiness of this transition that there may be times we are not even sure we exist! But no change in circumstances, however painful, can rob you of your worth, your possibilities, your dreams, your value, your vision, all you have struggled through and for, all you have learned and gained and given. *Nothing can diminish the miracle that is yourself.* You *are* a miracle! Do not regard yourself as less for a moment. You deserve your own highest respect, appreciation, understanding, forgiveness, and love. When we unconsciously take for granted the miracle of our own existence, we are guilty of "snacking on the sacrament." This forgetfulness may be humanity's greatest error. In dwelling on a mistaken belief that we are unworthy or unlovable, what have we forgotten? It is a sobering question, one we owe it to ourselves to remember to ask whenever we feel the grip of despondency tightening around our heart.

What does one do with a miracle that happens every moment of every day? We do not know, and that is the point. In this not knowing, this absence of conclusions, a natural roominess begins to occur within us, a roominess that is the mark of a great spirit, an open heart. This greatness was evident in the Warsaw Ghetto where, on a battered wall, someone scrawled what was later termed the "eleventh commandment:" *Thou shalt not despair!* Even in the worst of circumstances, how can we be so sure of the what and the why and the wherefore? We do not know what life is about, what we are about! It is all so astounding; can we not leave a little room in our suffering for the recognition that life comes and goes miraculously, prolifically, unencumbered by our plans and designs and nearsightedness and that tomorrow can bring anything? Our words deceive us: We say "life" and "consciousness" and "self," thinking that by naming things we have made sense out of the inscrutable. But the word is not what the word points to; for all our words, the seas churn, and the planets arc and spin through space, yet we do not understand even the first part of how or why or where it is all going. We can, even when we are in pain, take a moment to acknowledge the incomprehensibility within which we live and, at times, suffer. This acknowledgment is the first opening of awareness beyond the great constriction of the mind's all-too-tenuous certainties. We do not know enough, ever, to give up on the life that, still coursing through us, believes in us in its way.

Do not abandon the life within you. Do not identify with second pain. Refuse to take for granted the miracle of who you are. Remind yourself of your innate wonder, worth, and dignity. Bow before the greatness of yourself. Walk with your head as high as you can, reach out to others, and be patient. Recovery is already under way. /

GUIDANCE, COURAGE, SELF AS FRIEND

All our life, perhaps, we have overlooked the self's inherent wondrousness. As children, we may have felt the fascination of finding ourselves in a world, surrounded by things to see and hear and touch, astounded and delighted by our own toes. But as adults, we are far too busy with "practical" matters to stop and regard the miracle that is the self. We may have been taught that such high-flown "philosophical" ideas have little value in everyday life. What can one do with such thoughts, anyway? When asked, "What can you do with philosophy?" the phenomenologist Martin Heidegger answered: "Nothing, but if you are willing, perhaps philosophy can do something with you!" This suggests the sort of transformation that alone can restore the broken heart. And transformation is always at hand, which is to say, it is always found hiding in the obvious.

Ironically, even though our identity is greater than the mind can comprehend, we *think* we know who we are. In other words, we live not knowing that we don't know. There is a voice in our head, a voice that demands and insists, a voice that thinks it exists over and against the world, unto itself, as does the physical body.

We may think of this mind that seeks continually to exert its influence as the "willful-mind." While countless thoughts and feelings flow through this mind, it is clear upon even brief consideration that *we* are much more than any of these thoughts, more than even the "special" thought "I." In other words, this thought "I," while seeming to identify us to ourselves and others through its issues and arguments, its defenses, definitions, and desires, really has no discernible content or substance. It is an invisible point from which all we have mistakenly taken to be ourselves can be "owned." Of all the thoughts we think, this thought "I," which purports to establish our very identity, is the emptiest. As it turns out, we cannot think our being at all. It is too rich, too abundant, too overflowing in each present moment to be contained in any definition or thought. In the strictest sense, then, we are not who we *think* we are. It is only because we identify ourselves with this "I" thought, with the ever-separate, desiring, and contentious willful-mind, that we are able to take our true self utterly for granted. The true self resides in the heart, and, unlike the constricted, acquisitive, premeditating willful-mind, has an unlimited capacity for spacious awareness in the living present. We cannot continue to take this self for granted if we wish to recover.

> *The continuation of suffering rests on our continuing to identify with the willful-mind. Recovery begins when we begin to separate who we are from who we think we are.*

One of the most eye-opening experiences we can have is that of seeing through the camouflage the willful-mind has put in place to protect its authority and the seemingly vital interests it claims to serve. There is only one way to begin to see through what is false about us to what is true: We must learn to pay attention. Fortunately, we are not in the predicament faced by Dorothy and her improbable companions on their way to Oz, thrown by chance to search in a mysterious land for a wizard who is not real. To the contrary, once we open ourselves even to the possibility that our identity may be far greater than we had assumed, we find we are in familiar territory and that the self has many ways to guide and encourage us.

The word *courage* is fascinating. Originally, it meant "to be at heart with." Even today, when we want to inspire someone to be courageous, we say, "Take heart!" To be discouraged is to "lose heart" or be "disheartened." Frequently, we find the noblest states of the psyche associated with the heart. This etymological connection is an important one, for by *courage* we do not mean merely the ability to be or pretend to be brave.

> *Our first act of courage is to turn toward the heart, which is the home of the true self. Through this act of courage, we can begin to see what is real. Seeing and accepting what is real is the way out of suffering.*

Courage invites guidance, and guidance encourages us to be more courageous. In times of great suffering, and particularly when we have been abandoned, we may feel so alone that it seems there is no guidance, no support of any real substance anywhere. Despite powerful feelings of isolation and helplessness, understand that you are not alone, that these terrible feelings are merely feelings, and that guidance is available and at hand. Certainly, you are in need of en*courage*ment, of being heartened. Consider, then, that guidance is not only immediately available *but always has been.* It has been successfully called up within you on countless occasions. The ability to read the words on this page, for example, implies vast amounts of prior guidance *from within yourself,* for we do not learn directly from teachers, but from *recognizing* what our teachers are teaching us. This capacity for recognition occurs naturally within the self, in keeping with the "blueprint" it has for fulfilling its own possibilities. As the truisms state, the oak tree is in the acorn, the child is father to the man. There is, inherent in the self, an urge toward *purposeful movement.* This urge can be consciously experienced, once we become quiet and attentive, as specific guidance that directs and encourages self-expression and fulfills the promise of greater life. In fact, it is very hard to look anywhere and *not* see some form of guidance. In its broadest sense, guidance encompasses the order[1] of the physical world. The planets and stars are inherently guided in their paths, the seasons are guided in succession, the lungs are guided from breath to breath, the body's cells are guided to take in food and transform it into living tissue. In each case, a directing force—gravity, electromagnetism, biochemical interaction—fulfills the unique promise of what it directs. As the British philosopher David Hume pointed out, all around us we see this "perfect adaptation of means to ends": the bird's wings seem designed to take to the air, fish are born into a sea ready to receive and sustain them, our breathable atmosphere clings to the earth in direct proportion to the planet's mass and rotational speed. The world, in this sense, is a remarkable system of balances. It has integrity. Its parts fit with and belong to each other. As G. K. Chesterton said, frogs not only jump, they seem to like to.

Now, the inherent orderliness of the world is important to recovery for the abandoned person. Once we recognize that nature has a built-in guidance system, a time-and-space arena within which occurs an interplay of forces at both vast and minute levels, we can also recognize that this orderliness is not only "out there" to be observed in the physical world: It is also within us. It *includes* us. Our bodies move through space in response to our will; this movement requires no conscious control of neurons

[1]To be sure, there is also disorder in the world, especially the moral world. One cannot, however, consistently deny the order of the cosmos. Certainly, one can deny that this order proceeds from any intelligent, intending consciousness, but that is another matter. The very use of language implies a recognition of the order of things, such that those who deny order fall into a kind of philosophical hypocrisy. They cannot really believe what they claim, for if they do, there is no basis for their believing that their words still have the same meanings they had a few minutes ago. To deny order, then, is to presuppose it. In the history of modern philosophy, this is essentially the table Kant turned on Hume. That experience is ordered is, *a priori*, true; it cannot, without self-contradiction, be brought into question since questioning itself presupposes order.

firing, muscles contracting and releasing, or the hundreds of other autonomic functions that make intentional movement possible. Not only the body, but our emotions, thoughts, desires—all are guided by observable connections. All have a natural motion that is rich in purpose and inherently expressive. There is an inherent correspondence, an interconnection within which we, no less than the seasons, belong. Perhaps the sudden, clear-eyed gaze of a child elicits feelings of tenderness and innocence; the pounding heat of rush hour traffic frustrates us; the sunrise evokes feelings of wonder or reverence; the boss's egotism tests us. Feelings, while different for different people, are more or less appropriate.

We are not merely observers of the world's order, then, but participants in it. It involves us, permeates us. Within this order, things change and evolve in a magnificent dance of interconnectedness. We *cannot* be alone because to be alone is to be separate, and we cannot be separate, except inside the delusions of the willful-mind. The entire world takes part in this astonishing web of interrelationships. And it is our great possibility to take part in it consciously. The world moves in and through us, giving us a clue to the self we are beneath the self we have come to believe we are. Out of our participation in the world-order, we may expect that the earth we pollute will poison us, that the earth we nurture will sustain us. Every up has its down, every task its accommodation, every problem its solution. The most significant conclusion we can draw from this is that, despite how we may feel, we are not cut off. We live within a system that is by its very nature whole and supportive. It is remarkable that we have come to take this so utterly for granted. Order is not merely mechanical, it is personal. It operates at the very wellsprings of who we are and speaks to us from the heart. Here, order presents itself as guidance, offering us encouragement repeatedly in the form of a voice we generally ignore. We can, however, learn to hear it.

Hearing and trusting the self is tricky because we hear a lot of inner voices. Some call us to selfish, egocentric acts. Others may tell us we must be "good." Which one ought we to heed? The answer, which each of us must explore within the sacred temple of the self, is that we know more than we let ourselves discover we know. "I don't know" is often at bottom, "I don't want to know," a statement of our unwillingness to acknowledge what we know in our heart, rather than an admission of real ignorance. When we feel that knowing would cut us off from something we desire, or put us face to face with something we fear, we gag with great efficiency the intuitive self that knows only too well. This self has always been with us. It is at any moment our more promising, more expansive, more fully realized and richer identity, spontaneously sharing its clarity so that recovery and greater life can take place. *It is who we are when we are brave enough to face what is, as it is, without the distortions of ambition, fear, or preconceived notions.* We can hear it talking to us in our very hearts, beneath the voices of conditioning, beneath the many acquired prohibitions and insistences. We must be very still, very attentive to hear it, but it is not far away. It is there, as close as our own capacity for attentiveness and honesty. Socrates called this guiding voice his *daimon* and said of it that it always warned him when he was about to commit an error. In her brilliant work, *The Life of the Mind,* philosopher Hannah Arendt discusses the dialogue in which we may engage the inner voice as the "two-in-one":

> the duality of the two-in-one meant no more than that if you want to think, you must see to it that the two who carry on the dialogue be in good shape, that the partners be *friends.* The (inner) partner who comes to life when you are alert and alone is the only one from whom you can never get away—except by ceasing to think.[2]

We are beings who must return to inner dialogue in order to be on good terms with ourselves. As Arendt states:

[2]Hannah Arendt, *The Life of the Mind* (New York: Harcourt Brace Jovanovich, 1978), p. 188.

The guiding experience in these matters is, of course, friendship and not selfhood.[3]

This friendship with the self is actually the basis of that mature love we seek to cocreate with a partner. How sad that we do not first offer it to the self within us, do not seek it, listen to it, honor it, heed it, which is to say we do not yet belong to ourselves.

Acknowledging the true self and its authority through listening honestly can be terrifying because it is a call to discard familiar habits, no matter how inappropriate they may be. Paying attention to our own inner voice requires admitting and standing up to the many "recorded" voices that seek to invalidate it, which can threaten the decisions we've made about how to live our lives, decisions fixed by long practice, decisions we have either outgrown or never believed in to begin with. We are almost certain to find ourselves called upon to stop cooperating with some of these ingrained patterns, and this can be frightening. Listening to our heart may mean leaving a loveless relationship of convenience or dedicating ourselves to making a difficult partnership better, more honest, more loving. At first, paying attention to who we are can evoke feelings of extreme risk. Is it any wonder, then, that we spend so much time and effort avoiding it?

In the context of recovering from abandonment, the importance of befriending the self cannot be overemphasized. Many, if not most of us, have been deeply hurt and invalidated and, as a result, have low self-esteem. We may feel we are unworthy of love, and it is essential that we befriend the self if we are to do more with our lives than spend them alternately chasing and rebelling against the ever-changing states of our own willful-mind. Befriending the self is the beginning of the most important work you can do. Begin, therefore, to do it. Recognize that the self you really are is inherently valid, truthful, nurturing, expressive, mysterious, miraculous. Trust it. Have you not trusted so many things so much less worthy of your trust? Know that the

[3]Ibid, p. 189.

self is not by nature selfish, shrunken, rigid, or alone. It seeks to reach out, to experience, to learn, to understand, to create, to expand itself, to recognize itself in others through love—this wonderful self is given to each of us as a consummate trust. We would do well to consider that we have no right to denigrate it, to take it for granted, to violate or ignore its inner voice, to consider it worthless even if another has treated it so. Trusted, heard, and followed, this voice will connect us to ever-greater life, love, and fulfillment.

At present, befriending the self may mean nothing more than taking all the time you need to move *through* the pain. But ultimately it goes beyond the issue of pain. It means treating yourself as you would an excellent friend. It means believing in yourself and acting out of that belief. It means listening to yourself without the judgment and invalidation that may be as familiar to you as they are to anyone who takes the time to examine the contents and methods of his own mind. It means being kind to yourself in thought, word, and deed. It means refusing to torment yourself, refusing second pain. It means dwelling each day for a few minutes on the fact that the sacred circle of who you are embraces your life, your experience, your vision, your values, your love, your gifts, your talents, your purpose. It is the seed of all you can share with others. Befriending the self means at the very least suspending all the invalidating voices for a little while each day in order to practice inner listening, to practice gratitude and appreciation for the miraculous event of your being.

WHEN TALKING TO YOURSELF, IT'S NOT POLITE TO INTERRUPT

The self naturally offers us guidance and encouragement as we practice paying attention to what is going on within us rather than reacting to the endless inner stream of thoughts and feelings. Beneath this insistent parade, there is a vast and beautiful silence, a "citadel of peace," a lucid awareness of things as they are. It is here that recovery is nurtured. When we listen within for guidance, however, we usually find a mob of voices there. How can we break through the "static" of the willful-mind, its habits, fears, wishful thinking, conditioned responses, and reach the self "beneath" the self we have mistakenly taken ourselves to be?

The true self is always there. It presents itself when we make a little room for it in ourselves by sitting quietly in a nonjudging, self-loving watchfulness, letting the inner dramas continue in their course without reacting to them. We need only take a step back from the mind to calmly witness what is going on in our heart, which is the bodily focus of the true self. This self has been called the "subconscious," "voice of intuition," "higher power," "universal mind," "atman," "clear mind," "wisdom center," and many other names. It takes time to learn the "sound" of the self's wise silence; but, like a muscle, it strengthens and grows with use. During this exciting time, we can explore, experiment, and discover new abilities, as we did when we were children. While sitting quietly, paying attention, watching emotions come and go, and listening for this voice, we can apply the following criteria:

1. *The inner self advises for the common good; it does not play favorites.*

In this sense, the true self is not *impressed* (an interesting term) with all that seems so urgent to who we think we are—our worldly successes, prestige, title, appearance. While not aloof, it is not caught up in the emotional desperation that results when we overinvest ourselves in circumstances. This means the self addresses our real interests; it calls us to trust and act on the best in us. Because we are human, we are social beings, "herd" animals needing communion with our fellows. The human self seeks to expand. Eventually, it expands within and from the heart to include other selves, which then become part of the self. This is why the heart's instructions are never malicious or manipulative.

In this sense, while there are many, often conflicting minds in the world, there is only one heart. If we gain at the expense of someone else's well-being, our mind may be quite satisfied, even elated. But our heart cannot be. For the injury is inflicted against the self's larger possible identity, its fuller potential to be, as an expanding, inclusive entity. Arendt says about this:

> It is better to suffer wrong than to do wrong because you can remain the friend of the sufferer; who would want to be the friend of and live with a murderer?[4]

The self identifies with the one it has injured and its silent protests must be stifled if the egocentric course is to be continued. Thus, the heart's voice is indifferent to the demands of the willful-mind and is situationally compassionate; it directs us from outside the framework of willfulness, and therefore generally will not answer in terms of purely egocentric interests or events and circumstances, even those about which we have grown desperate. For example, "Will so-and-so come back?" is not likely to elicit a "yes or no" answer from the heart, though it certainly might. The unlikelihood of such a response hinges on the fact that such a question is almost always asked by the willful-mind, addictively; in other words, it's the wrong question as far as self-transformation and recovery are concerned. Rather than giving a "yes" or "no," either one of which would be misleading from the standpoint of real insight into the predicament, the true self might respond with a higher direction: "Let go, all will be well," or something similar, something that would encourage us to awaken to the present rather than remain sleeping in our painful dreams. We may tend to take such advice lightly because it does not speak in terms of our mind-dictated desires, but it is precisely this kind of guidance that, accepted and followed earnestly, can lead the way to self-transformation and release from suffering.

[4]Ibid, p. 188

2. *The inner self speaks in stillness.*

There is more to this than appears at first glance. The inner self speaks in stillness, when the body and mind are relaxed and receptive. It is never intrusive or overbearing; it does not shout. On the contrary, it whispers. It will even listen with unceasing patience to the willful demanding and begging we call "prayers," to our curses, our cries, our stories. In the sacred court of the self, our mind may plead its case as long as it wishes without interruption. But when we have had enough of the will-ful-mind's futile monologue, when we sit quietly within, main-taining, to whatever degree we can, an attitude of *receptivity,* then we extend an invitation to the heart to speak. This inner commu-nion comes of itself, we cannot *make* it happen. But we can gradually withdraw our attention from the demanding chatter of the willful-mind so that there will be a place for the heart to offer something new. The empty cup can be filled—another demon-stration of the Law of Opposites.

3. *The inner self is felt physically in the heart.*

Words are not merely spoken with the mouth. The word *logo,* commonly translated as *word,* comes from the Greek verb, *legein,* which means *to gather.* Uttering words involves a miracu-lous gathering: of air from the lungs, strength from the dia-phragm, thought from the mind, vibration at the throat site, and intention or meaning. The meaning of words is connected to various centers in the body, most notably the "head" or the "heart," though one may also "spill his guts" confessing, spout "hot air," "get it off his chest," "spit it out," and so on. We can quite literally "speak our heart" as surely as we can talk "through our hat" or "off the top of our head." It is intriguing that, by paying attention to this gathering aspect of the words we speak as we speak them, we can actually feel the intention behind our words emanating from a specific part of the body, again, usually the head or the heart. Only those words that speak to us from our own heart have the power to encourage. The self's true voice begins in the heart and seeks the heart in others. It is not intellectual, but compassionate; not theoretical, but practical; not analytical, but synthesizing; not clever, but wise. Hearing it, we are uplifted; there is an immediate and undeniable effect in the heart, which can be felt there.

When sitting quietly without external distractions and with eyes closed, we can begin to tune ourselves to the inner "airwaves" through which the heart and mind both "speak" to us and engage us in dialogue. It takes a little practice to learn to distinguish "heartspeak" from "headspeak," but the fact that their respective voices resonate in different parts of the body helps. Another important difference between them is that the mind sees differences, argues issues, defends heirarchies, is territorial about its "idea property." The heart, which is by nature open beneath the mind's barricades, sees unity, understands, identifies with others, forgives, and always chooses to affirm *life* rather than some idea of life.[5]

Here is a simple way to contact your true self for guidance or clarification: Sit quietly until you are calm. In that calm and without hesitation, ask your own heart the question that is in your heart to ask. Then listen. Eventually, a sense of lightness and understanding will "rise" in your chest and enter your consciousness in the form of an answer. This answer will not be a function of your own preconceptions or intentional willing, and your mind, upon hearing it for the first time, may raise its eyebrows. It will probably take a little time to develop this faculty, so don't lose heart. Sit calmly, with confidence that you are cultivating the kind of receptivity that will make it possible for you to hear the wisdom and compassion of your own heart. Gradually, you will develop an intuitive conviction of the reliability of information received from this center of silence. If you remain attentive, honest, and willing to even temporarily let go

[5]Dostoyevsky deals compellingly with this distinction in his short story "Dream of a Ridiculous Man."

of the demands arising out of the desires of your mind, you will get a response. The true self offers guidance from the deepest recesses of your own being. Take heart in it, follow it, trust it, continue to do so. In time—perhaps less than you imagine—it will guide you out of suffering.

Here is a meditative exercise you can do to experience the inner guidance available for the asking. Again, if you don't have success with it the first time, try it again later. Inner listening, like any other skill, must be developed through practice and an expectation of results. Have a friend read this exercise to you as you sit in a comfortable but alert position with eyes closed, or read it to yourself. Take several slow, deep breaths. Let thoughts and feelings come and go gently, simply watching them. Now, imagine yourself taking a shower, then getting dressed for an important appointment. This occasion is quite a special one: you are going to meet your true self. Breathe slowly. Let your eyes be still, do not try to see anything with them. Pay attention, watching thoughts, feelings, and bodily sensations rise, then fall away. Breathe gently. Relax your entire body, and sit quietly within. Now, imagine that you are approaching a cottage set in peaceful surroundings: a lush forest, by the ocean, or on a mountain, whichever you like. This is where your true self lives. You walk up to the cottage and knock on the door, feeling that you are about to see a dear friend who has wonderful news for you. Imagine the door opening to reveal your true self. Note what this self looks like; perhaps this is the first time you have ever met your inner guide. No matter how this guide appears, offer your greetings and your love. Now, sit down together. When you feel ready, openly present whatever is troubling you—a question, a problem, a fear. Breathe slowly and notice how the face of your guide glows with appreciation for your courage and honesty. The answer is now being presented to you as a gift. Take a few moments to receive it, to dwell on the answer. Breathe with the answer, slowly, gently. If its meaning is unclear to you, ask your guide for clarification. When you have received the answer, thank yourself, then sit quietly for a few more minutes. When you are ready, come back to the room and open your eyes.

DREAMS

A second form of inner guidance can be found in the dramas unfolding on the stage of the psyche while we sleep. They have tremendous power, not only symbolically, but as a practical storehouse of personal energy and a source of direction toward individual healing, purpose, and fulfillment.

One of the most common first reactions to being abandoned is an interruption of the sleep pattern. Insomnia, middle-of-the-night waking, fitful sleep, and nightmares are typical, sometimes all four in the same eight-hour period! There is no shortcut through this territory. Hours before dawn, when you awaken from an unsettling nightmare of rejection, when the tears are streaming hot along your cheeks and the ache of grief alternates with searing rage, you may feel there is nowhere to turn. *Another* night like this! How much can one take? There is the fear that if you do not sleep soon, you will go mad. Weeks, even months may go by in this way. You cannot remember what it means to sleep through a night, to wake up rested and refreshed.

If you go too long without sleep, physical exhaustion and the attendant psychological/emotional strain can aggravate the original problem, and your doctor may want to prescribe a mild, sleep-inducing drug temporarily. But again, real recovery requires self-transformation; it cannot be done with pills. An enormous amount of inner material is probably being made available to you for the purpose of your own healing, self-expansion, and the transcendence of suffering. Dreams are one form this material takes. Pay attention to them. You cannot tap this inner resource if you begin with an assumption that dreams are "merely" dreams, are not "real" or "relevant." Keep a "dream notebook" beside your bed and record your dreams in it upon waking. Be sure to leave yourself enough time in the morning to jot down as much of the dream as you can remember, and especially any element you recall as significant. It may be a single image, phrase, song lyric, or other fragment. Also, note the following: Date, Dream Summary, Question or Statement, and Meaning. Enter your comments under each heading without figuring them out beforehand, letting the pen or pencil "do the thinking" as you write. We are not interested in cleverness or censorship by the intellect. This should be largely a spontaneous process, uncolored by opinion or judgment. From time to time, go back and review entries over a two- or three-week period to see if there are recurring themes, images, or symbols that speak to you.

In general, there are three types of dreams that are particularly noteworthy:

1. Rejection or abandonment dreams

2. Instructional dreams

3. Precognitive/telepathic dreams

Naturally, many of the dream dramas you enact on the stage of sleep will "play out" the rejection. In these dreams, you may encounter monsters, accidents, or other violence, all expressing feelings of losing control. You may even find yourself reliving the same frustration, hurt, and desperation present in the waking experience; sometimes the details will be identical or very similar. As agonizing as it can be to have to undergo the injury repeatedly at a time when your body is crying out for rest, this is a vital emotional survival mechanism and need not be feared or resisted. It is natural; do not be concerned about it. Record whatever you remember of the dream in your notebook. Rejection or abandonment dreaming functions like a pressure valve. You will find these dreams diminishing as you practice watching the flow of your thoughts and feelings without identification and as the self shifts its focus from the willful-mind to the heart. As long as you are stuck in denial—for example, the insistence "This is not happening"—your psyche will attempt to present in dreams the reality denied in the waking state. *Denial fuels suffering.* We will deal with this at length later in our journey. Facing the denied reality in sleep allows you to discharge suppressed emotion and serves as an antidote for the poison of denial. Though painful medicine, it is effective. Remember, as the mind's demands defer to the reality of the situation, there will be less need for the self to use the dream-theater as a place to confront and accept reality.

The second type of dream offers instruction rather than simply reenacting the abandonment experience directly or indirectly. Such dreams typically produce some new insight that is experienced upon waking or later, during the day. There is a definite "Eureka!" quality. The dream's instruction may be connected with a symbol or double entendre: a stabbing in the back might signify a situation of betrayal, watching someone work a calculator might indicate a suspicion that the person is calculating and not to be trusted, a fear of fire might represent a fear of being fired, an I.D. bracelet might stand for one's identity, and so on. One need not consult commercial paperbacks on dream symbolism in order to understand one's dreams. The self is the best source of the meaning of its own, unique expressions. Instructional dreams can suddenly expose the falsity of the mind's selective conclusions, leaving one with a feeling of astonishment: "That's not how it was, that's only how I *thought* it was!" Often, they precede a recognition of how much one has "created" the beloved, who now stands forth in the light of his or her own demonstrated reality, something we will look at more closely later. Certainly there is much to be said for the idea that we do not really want to be with someone who is willing to leave us or who is chronically neglectful or abusive. If we consider the matter with a calm detachment and honesty, we will probably admit that we don't really want to be trapped in a situation of unrequited love.

Instructional dreams, then, open up insights, new perceptions of events viewed habitually through the sleepy eyes of the willful-mind during the waking hours. Visual fragments, surprising associations, pieces of sentences, song lyrics, all can serve to reorganize perception along clearer lines, loosening the grip of self-deception and suffering.

The third category is precognitive/telepathic dreams. This is a gray area, dealing as it does with extrasensory perception. Much research has been conducted both abroad and domestically since Dr. Rhine carried out his famous pioneering studies at Duke University. Most of us share a healthy skepticism about such matters, but we know that, in simple terms, radio communication can be received by an apparatus as unsophisticated as a piece of pencil lead moving across a razor blade. Who can say what feats of transmission and reception might be possible for electrical equipment as delicate and complex as the human brain and nervous system? Whether you believe in ESP or not, there is a convincing body of evidence for the authenticity of clairvoyance, clairaudience, and precognition—especially in situations where human awareness is energized by intense desire or love. If you have ever had such an experience, you will probably not be too concerned with evidence or proof; often they possess the same self-evident reality as normal, everyday experiences.

In dreams that you suspect are precognitive, you may foresee events unfolding in a certain direction and experience an unexplainable conviction that they will develop as seen. We are well beyond the domain of logic here; you may wish to trust this conviction and "wait and see" or simply chalk it up to indigestion. Interestingly, the ability to wait and see is itself healing. This is because impatience is characteristic of the willful-mind, which, as we have noted, has a strong tendency to control. Patience contradicts this tendency. The ability to wait and see how things will turn out affirms that one is connected with and receptive to reality, which naturally unfolds and changes over time. The willful-mind, on the other hand, must always have an answer now.

If a certain dream depicts reconciliation and a "happy ending," you may want to be more than a little skeptical. Such a dream might be nothing more than wishful thinking, the mind's willful denial of a reality that has thwarted its desires. Here again, personal conviction and a patient acceptance of the larger timing of things are central. While admittedly there is a risk in trusting this sort of conviction, it is not necessarily a bad one. Keep in mind that there is probably no important area of life that does not involve risk. By trusting a compelling precognitive dream, you are taking the chance that your inner understanding is worthy of trust, and this very trust may play a self-fulfilling role in the world of events. In any case, precognitive dreams offer the opportunity for some bold, inner exploration, the rebuilding of self-confidence, and the development of patience. When moving through this highly uncharted area of the psyche, an open mind seems like a good thing to take along. Record in your dream notebook any waking events that seemed to have been forecast by the dream. Do not force associations. Allow whatever wishes to present itself to do so.

HUNCHES

Hunches are another form of inner guidance from the self, coming in the form of suggestions for action that you may have a strong sense will improve things in some way. These intuitive suggestions are hardly limited to the racetrack. They are available in a wide range of situations, apparently in proportion to the amount of trust one is willing to place in them. Again, there is an element of risk involved here and it takes some time to gain proficiency in distinguishing bona fide inspiration from mere mental chatter or irrelevant urges. It is, however, telling that when we consider trusting our hunches, many of us immediately grow concerned about the damage we will do if they prove wrong. This is quite an editorial on the deep self-mistrust from which so many of us seem to suffer. Hunches spring from an inner vision that can encompass events in a way we cannot rationally explain, events that often affect us intimately. We do not need to understand how hunches work to at least experimentally open up to them, much as we do not need to understand the principles of internal combustion to drive a car from here to there. By disregarding them before the fact, however, we adopt an attitude that might well cut us off from a possible source of insight.

One way to tell a genuine hunch from inner static is to look for an element of surprise. Hunches have the unexpected in them. They often suggest something one would never have thought of "on one's own." Another guideline is to ignore a hunch unless it's strong and persistent. Trusted and followed, hunches can lead to new possibility, a resurgence of involvement, greater self-trust.

SPONTANEOUS CONVICTION

Whereas a hunch is a suggestion one may or may not follow, spontaneous conviction is experienced more as an imperative, a kind of knowledge one gains intuitively. It may come out of the blue, while one is watching television, for example, and is probably the most peculiar type of inner guidance. Suddenly, one simply knows the best course of action, understands the solution to the problem, intuits astonishingly specific details one could normally only know through direct perception or some other external source. Spontaneous conviction can make itself felt with practically irresistible force.

UNWILLED IMAGES

Typically, unwilled images show up in daydreams and more vividly during the pre-sleep period known as "the hypnogogic state." These, too, seem to come by themselves rather than being "thought up." They may be remarkably terse constructions of meaning that incorporate and summarize entire, complex situations, lending insight into deeper levels of a problem or indicating the direction of a solution. In this sense, unwilled images function in much the same manner as dream symbols: They demonstrate associations of meaning rather than logic. Sometimes, in the case of a strongly visually oriented person, they will appear as pictures on the "mindscreen" in response to a specific question. It may take some time before the image is grasped and understood by the analytical mind. Because of this, it is a good idea to keep an "image journal" in which to record these mental pictures and their significance. Keeping a pencil and pad near the bed will make it easy to jot down the details of the image before sleep comes and erases them from memory. In the morning, their significance will often be apparent.

Here is another exercise you can do to develop your awareness of your inner guide. As you get ready for the day, focus your awareness on the possibility that you will, in some new way, be guided to whatever is next for you in the healing process. As much as possible, get into the spirit of this. *Expect* guidance. We rarely find what we do not expect to find or are unwilling to find. It can be quite entertaining to playfully expect this guidance to reveal itself *symbolically,* knowing that it can reflect subtle and valuable information within the self, information generally overlooked by the habitual thinking of the mind. When you wake up, tell yourself that today is different because there is a *singular, undeniable moment of joy* waiting for you somewhere; you do not know where it is. This joy will be provided by your inner guide. As you go through the day, be aware that the joyful moment could present itself at any time. Tell yourself that, when it does appear, it will be clear, that it will make an undeniable claim on your attention. There may be many times during the day that you think of this exercise and suspect the joy to be hiding in this or that, but you will know if you are making it up, if you are forcing things rather than simply *receiving* the joy. There is no way to do this wrong. It is an exercise in receptivity. Disregard any concern about "getting it right," as though receiving joy were like answering a question on a test. *The joy will appear to come from the world, but will in fact be coming from your self.* Let the effort be effortless, the effort of playing. Notice things around you, how you feel about them, the subtle sensations moving through your body. Relax into the exercise. Remember from time to time to breathe deeply and gently as you go through the day open to the possibility of a joyful moment. When you receive the gift of this joyful moment, recognize that it is not coming to you from circumstances but is inherent in your increasing awareness of your true self. Beneath the endless stream of thoughts, feelings, habits, pains, pleasures, fantasies, and sensations, the joy is who you are.

SUFFERING

"The horror of that moment," the King went on, I shall never, never forget."

"You will, though," the Queen said, "if you don't make a memorandum of it."

—LEWIS CARROLL
Through the Looking-Glass

THE HABIT OF SUFFERING

BEAUTIFULLY EXPRESSING the transitory nature of human life, William Butler Yeats wrote in his poem "Nineteen Hundred and Nineteen":

> *But is there any comfort to be found?*
> *Man is in love and loves what vanishes.*
> *What more is there to say?*

Heart-awareness embraces the understanding that everything changes, that all we love will eventually pass on; the willful-mind resists this understanding, and it is this resistance that constitutes our suffering. In a world where the only constant is change, where what we love vanishes, a world in which we have already endured so many disappointments and losses, we can only have peace by living from within a deep letting-go, moment to moment. Without this letting-go, this cooperation with the forces of change, we are at the mercy of the controlling mind, which can never fulfill us with its dreams of a lasting circumstantial happiness. We may as well stand in the middle of a rushing river and try to stop its powerful current with a sieve, so impossible is the task the poor willful-mind has set for itself: to stop the miraculous motion of each moment, to control and direct life while all the while standing apart from it and resisting in order to feel its own false sense of security strengthened. But the payoff of resistance is short-lived; this may be the predicament Yeats was noting: not merely that a lifetime is, after all, brief, but that what we "love" begins to vanish from the very moment we attain it. The willful-mind is profoundly fickle; it is geared for disappointment, discontent, and that restless pursuit of conditions in which there can be no real peace. Clearly, when we fail to get what we want, we suffer. Even when we succeed in attaining what we want, the sweetness in the mind is bittersweetness: Either we fall into the seemingly inevitable worry and fear that we will lose what we have attained, or desire pulls us in another direction and we again find ourselves separated from our imagined happiness. Losing and winning are thus the "chains of iron, chains of gold" in which the mind shackles the heart. *Whether we succeed or fail, as long as we are identified with the willful-mind, we resist life. And to resist life is to suffer.*

Life flows in its course regardless of the willful-mind's inherent fear and craving, and as we take a step back onto the bank of the river, where things are more peaceful, we come to understand that the mind's resistance and willfulness can never lead to sufficiency, that nothing can be sufficient but the present, and that the present cannot be found by the mind that is ever off in the past or the future, ever seeking to control. The living present *cannot* be controlled; it is too abundant, too overflowing in its very sufficiency. And all that keeps us from entering into the joyful awareness of simple, here-and-now being is the masquerade of separateness. Identification with the desires of the mind creates suffering because the mind believes this masquerade, and separateness means being cut off, left out, forsaken. Thus, a great division is set up within the self by the mind's willfulness. Long before a partner abandoned us, we abandoned ourselves. We learned to live in separateness: separateness from the living present, from our heart, from the joy of being. To be identified with the willful-mind is to suffer, though most of the time we accept

this suffering as normal and move through our days un[
how deeply absent we are from life and how much grief we carry
in us as a result. This is the tragedy, that we do not even know
how much we are suffering until our suffering reaches the threshold of crisis, whereupon we run around hoping God is real and
that our desperate prayers will be answered. Sooner or later, the
mind's posing evaporates in the face of what is real. Perhaps
someone we love dies, or leaves us, or a test comes back from the
lab with the worst possible results. At such a time, we have no
idea in the world of where to turn, because there is nowhere in
the world to turn. Only the heart can guide us out of the suffering
inherent in a world where what we love vanishes. When the
mind is forced to look in the mirror of its own powerlessness,
nothing can help us but the time we have given to practicing love,
to identifying with the spaciousness of the heart, to letting go and
simply living, here and now.

The suffering we carry, whether we are aware of it or not, has
many dimensions. Our heart has been broken, in fact, by innumerable experiences over the years. Being left by a partner may
have opened a major fissure, a fault line in the heart, but as we
become aware of the heaviness we feel in the chest area, we
recognize a myriad of secondary and tertiary cracks: all the moments we felt abandoned, humiliated, inadequate, guilty, fearful,
misunderstood; the thousands of times a violent thought or feeling hammered within us, driving the wedge of separateness
deeper; the countless moments we wanted to speak our heart, to
say "I love you," but could not find the courage to let love over-
take us, to give up control; the dear ones we have lost to death
or estrangement and the ones we know, in our heart, we must
lose one day; all the times a loving gesture by us went unnoticed
or unappreciated; the stowed grief of disowned compassion for
the thousands in our world who go to bed hungry every night;
the switched-off remorse over soldiers who went off to die in war
and those we did not welcome home; and on and on. There is no
room in the mind for so much grief! Better to simply encase the

heart in armor than give up our false sense of separateness and control, and melt into so much sorrow.

As we allow ourselves to enter into this suffering, tremendous grief wells up in us, and, especially if we forget to be compassionate with ourselves, we may fear we will be lost in it. Sometimes this comes as a tangible fear that we will spin totally out of control, that we will go crazy or disappear. This feeling is a natural part of recovery and will pass. It results from releasing the constrictions and denials that give the willful-mind its sense of security and control. Gradually, we begin to "fit" into this new, more expansive identity. We experience the heart's tremendous roominess, its limitless accommodation for the living present. And we come to recognize that we have an identity above and beyond the suffering, as the calm, gentle watcher. This separating out of the self from the inner turbulence with which it is so identified is a milestone on the path of recovery. By allowing the turmoil of long-denied grief to surface with a calm, steady detachment, we see that it does not have as much to do with who we are as we thought, that who we are is much more the loving roominess within which the chaos is admitted, accepted, allowed to come and go. We start shedding our identification with our suffering as a snake sheds an old skin, slowly but inexorably. This process does not appear to be easy for the snake, and it is certainly not easy for us. But we must go through our suffering, experience it with the light touch of the heart in order to become aware of our wholeness. Continued denial will only postpone the payment of debt and, therefore, the living of life. Ultimately, we must let go of all of it, must accept it into the spacious heart and experience it, must let our life "pass before our eyes," which is to say our heart's eyes. We must even make room to accept our resistance. If, for example, we wake up in the middle of the night, longing for our partner, we need only become centered, take a few slow, calming breaths, and begin to note the particulars of what is before us: the aching feeling in the chest and stomach, the emptiness of the bed beside us, the way the pillow is lying at a slight angle, the soft light coming through the curtains from the

streetlamp, and so on. Simply noting, with gentle a
respect. This becomes our "daily bread," that each
practice opening, taking whatever is before us into ...
without interfering, judging, denying, or clinging. In this way,
we take a stand in the heart and let the river wash over us. We
hurt; we see ourselves falling out of our heart and back into the
mind; we note that we have allowed frustration to claim us once
again; we become aware that we are racing off into the past or
the future; we watch desire arise, insist, abate—and through it
all, we return to the heart, acknowledge whatever is present,
accept what is beyond our control, bow to it. In this way, day by
day, moment by moment, we extricate ourselves from self-com-
bat and suffering, and emerge increasingly into the living present.

The willful-mind is incessantly in a state of desire, planning
some way to get or avoid this or that, thinking that doing so will
bring happiness. Desire is its vocation, lack its currency. *The
willful-mind focuses on what it does not have, which is why it is forever
in flight from the living present.* Our desires project us restlessly
into the future in pursuit of something; therefore, to the extent
that we live through our desires, we are not living here and now.
Because the willful-mind habitually misses the present, which
alone is real, it is embroiled in insecurity, an insecurity that
intensifies as we learn that things are rarely what we imagine
they will be. When the mind succeeds in attaining the object of
its desire, dissatisfaction sets in quickly because the real relief of
getting what we want is in the *momentary cessation of desire itself,
and the corresponding relief from the tension of self-separateness,* not in
the object attained. The willful-mind never comprehends that
the heart of the matter has nothing to do with fulfilling this desire
or failing to do so, that desire itself is the culprit. Along these
lines, George Bernard Shaw wrote in *Man and Superman*, "There
are two tragedies in life. One is to lose your heart's desire. The
other is to gain it."

We have identified ourselves for so long with the mind's
desires, its fulfillments and frustrations, that we are driven by

them and in our "pursuit of happiness," actually demonstrate all the characteristics of *addiction.* Here, we must face a hard truth, but doing so is essential to recovery:

Suffering is addiction to pain.

Caught in the trap of its own, self-defeating methods, the suffering mind insists, "Look what the world has done to me! My life is ruined! I am alone!" In such a condition, we are locked up, rigid, constricted. Our awareness has become clenched, a fist rather than an open hand; consequently we can receive nothing but the second-pain loops of our own distress. Because any addiction ties us up in destructive patterns, we are closed to the present moment and cannot receive the only life we have: the here and now.

Every addiction is based on the denial of what the addicted person knows, in his heart, to be real. When we are addicted, we refuse to accept things as they are because we have identified so much with our desire for them to be different. My friend Saviz expressed this well in the context of how we create others in our own image: "You have this quality, not because you have it, but because I want it!" We feel that who we are hangs in the balance of whether or not we attain what we mistakenly call our "heart's desire," and denial allows the willful-mind to continue the chase even in the face of clear evidence that what we seek either is not available at this time or would, despite its appeal, only add to our misfortune. Such is the power of denial. The late-stage alcoholic who takes "just one" is convinced that this time it will be different until he wakes up in a detox ward again, with delirium tremens. The compulsive gambler who places the rent money down on a long shot believes that this time his number will be the winning one. The woman whose husband has beaten her for years tells the doctor setting her broken arm, "He's really a very nice man. . . ." In order to justify whatever our "fix" is, we convince ourselves what we know in our heart is patently untrue. And when reality comes sweeping down upon us, we suffer.

Having been abandoned by someone we love, we become susceptible to many beliefs based on denial, such as the following:

> Life cannot be good now that my partner is gone.
> I know my partner loves me and is coming back.
> I can't go on without my partner.

These are all dramas of the willful-mind; all contain tacit desires, all are focused in the future, all involve flight from the immediate present, and herein, even more than in the mind's presuming to know what will be, lies the denial. We cannot break an addiction as long as we deny the present, which is exactly what we do when we race off into the mind's judgments and conclusions. Recovery begins with a *willingness* to attend to and accept the present reality, this moment, now, whatever it includes. Our unwillingness to accept the present moment as it is keeps us suffering. Reality is the present; to see reality, we must begin where we are and take an honest look at our suffering itself. We may feel we are victims of our pain, of fate, of someone else's actions, but have we in some way been perpetuating our suffering?

Have you fallen into a habit of suffering? When was the last time you felt fully alive? Have you been stuck in a pattern of dissatisfaction? How do you feel when you get up in the morning: quietly grateful for the moment of waking or burdened by the prospect of facing another day? Are you having the same sorrowful conversations with friends, over and over again, about your having been left? Reaching out to others is a double-edged sword: It is a powerful healing force if those to whom we turn for support are clear enough in advance not to collude with us in our misery.[1] If, on the other hand, the support we get reinforces our sense of ourselves as victims of circumstances, it can be a great hindrance. The sympathy and often biased agreement of friends and family can feel vindicating, but it only keeps us

---

[1] Alcoholics Anonymous and other self-help groups that deal with overcoming addictive habits call this kind of support "tough love."

stuck. Any advice that does not encourage us to look within ourselves, to honestly confront whatever role we may be playing in perpetuating our own suffering, will ultimately work against us. Addictively seeking out justifications for our resistance to what is happening cannot bring an end to suffering. Such seeking is a kind of emotional "mainlining;" it only aggravates the problem by feeding the false self, the willful-mind, one of whose favorite roles is that of the victim. A vicious cycle is established: We recoil from some painful reality, deny it, seek out support for the denial, then find ourselves suffering the resistance, contradictions, and futility inherent in any denial of what is real. We suffer both the original "debt" of pain and the accrued "interest" of suffering. The more we seek endorsements for our denial, the more suffering tightens its grip. Only when we reach a point of exhaustion may we suddenly realize that we must go the other way, that we must pay attention to what is hurting us rather than push it away, that we must accept it, feel it in its very presentness to be free of it. Here, we come upon a landmark on the way to recovery:

> *Suffering is not the same as pain. It is possible to be in pain without suffering. Suffering can end even when pain has not ended yet.*

In common usage, being in pain is the same as suffering. But these two are profoundly different. Pain is a natural, spontaneous reaction to conditions that violate us in some way—physically, emotionally, morally, or spiritually. Those aspects of reality that we call "painful" rise and fall within the immediacy of awareness, that is, they are "given" to us from time to time. Suffering, on the other hand, is the willful-mind's reaction to pain. It has its roots in desire, in the insistence that things be other than they are. When we identify with our pain, we find we are unable to make room, through loving awareness, for the pain to simply come and go. Instead, we magnify it through our very resistance. Pain may be part of the present; suffering is a flight from the present. When pain happens to be part of what is real in the moment, the denial of pain is the denial of reality, and the denial of reality is almost a clinical definition of madness. When we are living in the willful-mind, we *are* mad. Sanity comes from living in the heart, in a loving awareness and acceptance of what is, even if this means letting go of how we would like it to be. This brings us to the second landmark on the way to understanding suffering:

Suffering cannot stand in the face of what is real.

The ancient alchemists reportedly could transmute base metal into its purest form, gold. Similarly, we can transmute suffering into "ordinary" pain through our willingness to see what is really there. This path leads to deep healing for the heart torn by abandonment. By accepting what is real and relinquishing denial, we can return to life. Choosing to accept what is real may still leave us with pain, but this is vastly better than enduring a state of chronic suffering in addition to the pain. We cannot control the person who left us. But we can choose simply to let ourselves be sad about our loss without identifying with this sadness to the extent that we feel our very self is at stake. Without this identification, the sadness can be just sadness; it does not have to become depression, desperation, or a chronically self-inflicted trauma.

As we examine what is real, we may be surprised to discover some of the specific ways we have made a habit of suffering. The word "masochist" is a distasteful one—certainly we would not apply it to ourselves. It can, therefore, be quite a shock when we realize that we may have willfully held onto pain as a result of deep, unexamined convictions we have about who we are and how the world is, convictions that make pain a fix and the continuation of pain unavoidable. Sitting quietly with our suffering, noting it with compassion from the heart, we may discover subtle motivations for holding onto pain. Listed below are eight of these. If you recognize your own emotional motivations in any of them, congratulate yourself for your honesty. The willingness to recognize and accept yourself as you are eases the constriction that is characteristic of any addiction. It is an important step forward on the road to recovery.

1. Being right: Especially if we grew up in a home where being wrong meant being blamed, we may place extraordinary importance on being right. Under the surface of perfectionism often lurks a deep need for safety and a fear of rejection that can prompt one to "cut off his nose to spite his face," to inflict pain on himself and others rather than admit error and relinquish the willful-mind's claim to absolute authority. Long ago, many of us were taught that there was no room for error. This rigidity cut us off from the heart's natural spaciousness, patience, and forgiveness. Now, we may simply want so much to avoid being blamed that we will dig in our heels and refuse to quit a position we know in our heart is self-defeating. As long as we insist on justifying our madness in this way, we will continue to suffer. We are especially vulnerable to this indulgence if we have been left by someone, because it is very easy for us to feel sorry for ourselves when someone we love has left us. Self-pity is a form of being right in which we maintain the posture of the victim, often secretly or openly condemning the one who has put us in this terrible position. The greater reality, accessible from the heart, is that, quite frankly, it is not easy to be the leaving party either, and, in any case, our having been left does not mean we are no longer capable of living boldly, courageously, and gratefully.

2. Lack of self-worth: We may believe or fear that we are unworthy to receive what we say we want; perhaps we feel that getting it would be embarrassing or humiliating in a way we are unwilling to accept. In cases of extremely poor self-esteem, we might even believe we deserve to be in pain. If so, we are likely to experience pain as a confirmation of our sense of unworthiness. This is the old routine, "I wouldn't want to belong to any club that would have somebody like me as a member." We end up vindicated but lonely as we continue to do time in the solitary confinement of the willful-mind's unloving self-judgments. Here, the mind may repeatedly set up rejection scenarios that seem to confirm its self-defeating belief, it is skilled at creating what it fears as well as what it desires, through self-fulfilling situations we experience as happening *to* us rather than *through* us. We may, for example, behave irresponsibly on the job, come in late, perform duties halfheartedly, then when we are fired, lament: "I knew I'd be fired from that job; nobody really liked me there." Low self-esteem will eventually undermine any relationship in exchange for an impoverished vindication. Probably the ultimate example of this sort of logic is the case of the hypochondriac who left instructions in his will for his headstone to read, "See, I told you I was sick."

3. *A sense of being alive:* Especially if we have shut down our ability to feel and respond to the joys and pains of the living present, we may need to suffer to have a sense of being in our body at all, of being real. When we've been numb for a long time, pain gives us a sense of being alive. It seems better to feel bad than to feel nothing.

4. *A sense of security:* In a paradoxical way, suffering can be comfortable simply because it is familiar. What is familiar seems safe. Suffering can serve to protect us from the emotional risk of venturing out into the unpredictable present, where we might be called upon to love, to give up control, to be vulnerable.

5. *An excuse for laziness:* Suffering allows us to feel justified in our anger, in complaining, in blaming others, and, therefore, in avoiding the responsibility to open ourselves to a joyful, healthy life, grounded in the present. People usually don't make demands of us when we are hurt or "ill" or "fragile." We can, in subtle ways, recruit those who are willing to play opposite us in the victim/rescuer melodrama. By suffering, we can sidestep responsibility for our own growth and transformation.

6. *Pain as "normal":* We can be addicted to a certain level of dramatic tension. It seems that a great number of us have never seen the natural balances of a healthy awareness modeled, either by parents or partners. When we have remained for too

long in the habit of identifying with the mind's dramas, balance and moderation feel foreign. We are not comfortable being comfortable. Pain becomes "normal," and we seek it out to relieve the peculiar tension that accompanies the absence of suffering. This is a form of "I'm so used to being nervous that when I'm calm, it makes me nervous," which in reality, is far from funny.

7. *Avoiding and controlling others:* Our desire to avoid pain generally compels us to avoid those who are in pain. This works the other way around, too: By staying in pain ourselves, we can keep others at a distance and therefore control them. Behind this motivation is the fear of intimacy and ultimately a fear of our own heart, of love. Perhaps getting close in the past meant being left or being hurt badly in some other way. Those who present to us the prospect of emotional closeness evoke in us all the old, accumulated fears. We may resort to suffering as a way of keeping them at a safe distance, even while sending out conflicting messages inviting intimacy. Many undermine a love because of a deep fear of losing it. This is like the child who, seeing the bully approach to knock down his building blocks, knocks them over himself, thereby denying the bully the satisfaction. Addiction to pain can lead us to so expect being hurt that we create the very thing we wish most to avoid.

8. *Alleviating guilt:* We may also suffer because we have seen others in our family suffer and do not wish to feel the guilt of the disloyalty that would be involved in living joyfully when they do not. This has been termed "survivor guilt" and has been observed in those who have lived through the Holocaust and other wartime experiences. Outside the sphere of such trauma, this guilt is usually the result of secret rules and mandates at work in dysfunctional families, rules and mandates that condemn each member to stay within the sick system. To become healthy is to become disloyal, and it is easier to suffer than to face and deal with such feelings of disloyalty and guilt.

In all of the above reasons for suffering, the payoff is invisible to the sufferer because denial is at work. Ironically, we practice denial initially in order to cope with a situation so adverse that denial has survival value. The child with a violent mother, for example, cannot accept that his mother hates him, that she wants to kill him with her anger. We deny in order to avoid the real pain of a reality too painful to handle. But denial is resistance and resistance eventually only intensifies our pain, creating a vicious cycle. When exhaustion has brought the willful-mind to an impasse, we have the opportunity to open to something beyond the willful-mind. Slowly, we become aware of our heart's connection with the simple, living present and begin to sense that the way out of suffering is to stop running; to honestly acknowledge our desires, addictions, and dependencies, including the painful realities of the present situation; to "embrace our thousand angels and thousand demons," as Buddhism teaches; and to do nothing for a while but sit quietly and observe it all, each moment, from the heart. This sitting with oneself as one might sit with an old friend—not giving counsel or asking questions, but simply offering the compassion of being *with*—can be an especially powerful tool for transformation when we are truly weary of suffering, when we are at a complete loss as to what to do. In this "not-doing," the spiraling cycle of pain/denial/suffering has a chance to slow down, to become apparent to itself. The self is given a moment outside the momentum of the willful-mind's addiction. Something new is free to show itself. An open place of gentle awareness is recognized in the heart, a spaciousness that relaxes the fists, the clenched teeth, the tense jaw.

Facing up to our denial means being deeply honest about how we have been deluding ourselves. This is not easy; we cling to our delusions greedily and the camouflage of the willful-mind can be insidious and persistent. We are all identified with the mind to some degree and are usually proud of it: We are the "captain of our fate, the master of our soul," even if it kills us and other people in the bargain. To make matters worse, denial seems to follow an inverse principle. The more sensitive we are to pain and the more we seek to avoid it, the more tenaciously do we cling to denial of the painful reality. In other words, the more we seek to deny the pain in a given situation, the more we will suffer. By becoming aware of our pain, admitting it, feeling it intimately—but, most of all, not denying it—we place ourselves in cooperation with the Law of Opposites: Yielding overcomes resistance. Painful conditions will pass in due course if we refuse to conspire with the willful-mind by denying them, if we refuse to support second pain. Once we see this, we may wonder how we ever could have contributed so energetically to our own undoing.

Here is an exercise that will help you to feel pain as "ordinary" pain, without reacting to it, without dramatizing it into suffering: Sit quietly and take several slow breaths, relaxing the body. When you are calmly centered, imagine something about your former partner that you miss, perhaps a physical feature or mannerism. This thought may fill you with anxiety or grief or anger, but do not resist. Let the details into your heart, along with any memories associated with them. Feel the ache that enters the chest area with this recollection; do not resist it. If tears come, let them. Do not run from the bad feeling into feeling bad about feeling bad. You have been running long enough. Take a slow, deep breath, acknowledging the pain, then release the breath and imagine that you are releasing the pain along with it. This pain you feel is part of your life right now; it is not your whole life. Sigh again. Breathe. Release the breath, the pain. Accept the moment as it is. Make a place in your heart for it. No more fighting, no more resistance. You are entitled to rest from suffering into the simple sadness of loss. Let it come, let it go. Feel, breathe, sigh. Into the heart. The moment, even of pain, is sufficient when we accept it exactly as it is.

WILLFUL-MIND: THE MONKEY TRAP

The willful-mind is like fire: restless, ever-changing, never still for a moment. The heat it gives off is the heat of desire, and it consumes our very awareness like a flame consumes oxygen. As soon as any object of desire is attained, it begins to turn to ashes, and the mind must move on to new fuel. This is its nature, and the mind can be an invaluable servant. The trouble starts in our identifying ourselves with this mind, in believing it is who we are, at which point it becomes our master. Then it is we ourselves who are on fire. Consumed by our suffering and our separateness, we may live our lives feeling a deep undercurrent of sorrow, alienation, fear, constriction, homesickness. Especially in a world where we are technologically capable of utterly destroying ourselves, it is more important than ever for us to understand that identification with this fire can be fatal.

When identification with the willful-mind is strong enough, desire becomes addictive and suffering results. A story that powerfully illustrates this self-destructiveness inherent in suffering tells of a group of island natives who are hunters. One of their favorite prey is monkeys and they have an ingenious trap to catch them in large numbers. They take a coconut, cut a hole in it just large enough to accommodate the average adult monkey's hand, and hollow it out. Some rice or fruit is placed inside the coconut as bait. Then, a vine is tied through another, smaller hole in the opposite side of the coconut and the end of the vine secured. The hunter moves off to wait some distance from the trap.

Sooner or later, a monkey approaches the coconut, sees the rice, reaches inside, and grabs. Immediately, he is caught, for the hole, cut just large enough to allow him to insert his hand, will not release his *fist*. He panics and thrashes about, closing even more tightly the hand that, if he would but open it, would give him his freedom instantly. As long as he holds onto the rice, he is captive. The more tightly he holds, the more tightly he is held by the trap. Hearing the commotion, the hunter returns—and the story ends.

Here we have a striking analogy for the difference between pain and suffering: Often we hold in our hands the power to release ourselves, yet the desire to avoid pain, to deny it, to get away from it is so strong that we allow ourselves to be caught in enormous suffering and vastly greater misery than the entire process is intended to avoid. We become our own hunter and our own prey; we trap ourselves. The monkey's addictive desire is his compulsive craving for the rice. Refusing to let it go, he falls into a kind of denial, failing to see the reality of easy escape, and his fate is sealed by the second pain of panic.

Now, let us suppose the hapless monkey had the power of heightened self-awareness for a single moment. He could stop, look, listen, reflect on what is happening and, most importantly, on his unwitting but decisive participation in the self-destructive process. He could "step outside" the self-escalating horror of desire and panic, which would bring into relief the mechanics of his trapped hand. He would realize that if he would just relax and open his hand, he could pull it out through the hole as easily as he pushed it in—an obvious fact once the panic, the tension, and the attachment to the prize are suspended for a moment. In that reflective pause, the obvious could show itself, and it would show itself as something entirely new. He could open his hand. He could live.

It is the same with us. *Our suffering masks the tolerability of our pain.* It transforms the hurtful into the hideous, the tragedy into catastrophe. It locks us into the drama of our predicament, and we lose sight of the heart's great roominess and receptivity. Though we may fear our pain will kill us, by opening ourselves to it, we step into the domain of our natural power and resiliency and come through more alive, not less.

Again, pain may be there (the monkey doesn't get the rice). But we can live with pain. Pain is inevitable for creatures who are sensitive, aware, conscious. Because we are such creatures, we can remind ourselves that pain will pass, that we can live with it. Pain is part of life, and when we feel our pain as pain, we are alive. But when we suffer our pain, we are not yet fully alive.

THE COW AND THE BARN

By letting our pain come and letting it go, by allowing it to run its course rather than holding onto it, we move, to whatever degree we can, beyond the constriction of the mind's willfulness and begin to embrace larger realities. When we are stuck, of course, such terms as "greater reality" can seem of little value. But even though we may not, strictly speaking, *know* what it means, we can open ourselves up to a new awareness, a new experience of ourselves beyond the mind's knowing. We do this by letting go, by moving in directions opposite to those dictated by suffering: We let go rather than cling, we watch the inner turmoil rather than identify with it, we reach out to others rather than curl up and hide in isolation, we feel our pain rather than push it away. *Moving in the opposite direction plays an important role in breaking the cycle of addictive reaction.*

To illustrate: Imagine a cow, six feet from and facing an open barn door. The cow has a rope tied around its neck. Visualize yourself taking up the rope and attempting to pull this half-ton creature, which most definitely does not want to oblige you, into the barn. You are free to pull your brains out. The cow is dug in and won't budge. This is analogous to the passion with which we try to drag into being events that reality, for one reason or another, is not interested in helping us with. Now, imagine letting go of the rope, walking around behind the cow, taking its tail, and pulling it *away* from the barn. Feeling this new tug from the back and contrary by nature, it now marches promptly *into* the barn. Or maybe it doesn't. In which case, there you are, with the cow, catching your breath.

This symbolizes what happens when we let go of what seems so urgent in order to open ourselves to a greater reality than the one in which we are stuck. We must let go of the rope before we can take the cow by the tail and try something new, something that understands there is no point in fighting the cow's contrary nature (painful reality). We can do this when we recognize that our insistence is self-defeating and accomplishes nothing but our exhaustion. By letting go of the rope, we "make room" for something different, a different reality, to happen. Note that in real practice, even before we can "let go of the rope," we must make room *within ourselves* by surrendering our delusion about being able to pull the cow, headfirst, into the barn. It is essential to remember that, from the wilfull-mind's point of view, *letting go of the rope feels like losing everything, perhaps even like losing our identity.* The true self within us knows, however, that we must acknowledge and accept reality rather than fight it and that our ability to do so is liberating.

We may take heart from the fact that our suffering, which seems so fathomless and chronic, is based on nothing more than a false sense of who we are and that, by becoming aware of our real identity, we can escape suffering with or without a partner. This transformation is largely a matter of paying attention to our desires long enough to recognize whether they are in accord with the timing of the present, and, if they are not, of lovingly noting them, taking them into our heart with compassion, and letting them go. Once we have done everything in our power to persuade our partner to come back and have failed, we can move in the opposite direction: We can release ourselves from the willful-mind, recognizing that life is bigger than our present idea of what life should be. This means that we are willing to yield to something greater than our own will, something we can only remotely sense, something that waits, perhaps, just beyond the mind's strategies, to embrace us. Life and the gladness of being alive can come to us quite unexpectedly if we have let go of all that keeps it at bay, if our arms are open to receive it, not closed in a sorrowful self-embrace.

DELUSION: TWO CLASSIC EXAMPLES

In our heart, we are already recovered, already whole. All that is needed is for our awareness to expand so we can consciously experience our own natural joy, grace, and sufficiency in the living present. *We do not need to change ourselves, only our awareness of ourselves, and this makes a real difference in terms of our approach to recovery.* Like the sun, which is shining all the time regardless of the earth's rotation or the presence of heavy cloud cover, our "original" identity is spontaneously bright, open, generous, wholeheartedly alive. It has only been obscured by the mind's delusions. We must become aware of these delusions in order to go beyond them to who we really are. Here are two examples of how the willful-mind concludes that recovery is not possible:

1. "I don't know *how* to let go of this. I *am* in
    terrible pain! How can I make it different than it
    is?"

2. "I'll try to stop suffering."

The first of these is pure willful-mind, for which *knowing* has great significance. The willful-mind always has good reasons. It has evidence; it is right. "Knowing," however, is only an impressive word it uses to describe its habit of drawing conclusions, a habit through which it imposes its judgments on the present and in so doing, misses the present, which is the only place it can be liberated. The willful-mind is convinced that knowing how to do something has everything to do with doing it. In certain areas of life, this is true, namely technical knowledge and craftsmanship, but generally, and especially where living in the living present is concerned, knowing how is simply not relevant—except perhaps inversely: We come to our heart more by accepting how little we know, by relinquishing our conclusions in deference to the miraculous present. If a man sat on the couch and seriously believed he had to know how to move across the room before getting up and doing it, he would never get up. Without his knowing, intention is somehow translated into neural impulses and his muscles somehow respond appropriately. Transforming food into living cells is another example; it is fortunate for us that our body does not first consult us to see if we know how this is done before going ahead and doing it. We do not know, ultimately, how we breathe and think, how we feel, how we heal from sickness and injury, how we love, how we put together a sentence and speak it without having in mind all the exact words we're going to say. Yet, without knowing, we manage to do these things quite naturally and adequately to the needs at hand. Similarly, we can recover without knowing how. It is given to us to be able to pay loving attention and, eventually, to find out that we *are* the spacious, spontaneously joyful awareness within which all thoughts, feelings, and phenomena rise and fall away, each moment.

Another aspect of this first delusion is the idea that there is anything to "make different." Again, here we see the restlessness of the willful-mind: it is always doing something, never simply paying attention to what is already done, already given. The hardest thing for the willful-mind to grasp is that there is nothing to do. The heart is already open. Recovery is possible in each moment because the essence of our identity is wholeness and awareness, not separateness and reaction. When we are having a vivid nightmare, we may believe, in the heat of the action, that we must slay the monster; swim up through a thousand, murky fathoms; or leap across a fiery chasm to safety. In fact, we are already safe, in bed, sleeping. We need only wake up and realize it, and the nightmare is over.

The second delusion is subtler. "I'll try" means "I'd like to recover, but there are greater forces that may make the project fail, despite my efforts." "Trying" is an excuse made before the fact that allows us to be halfhearted while convincing others not to think badly of us. This is a denial of the self-as-heart, however, because the heart is not halfhearted; its responses are appropriate and competent to the needs of the moment because they are made in the awareness of what is real. Consequently, the heart does not focus on excuses, it does not "try." In every area of life we consider essential, we do not bother with "trying." We get up in the morning, eat meals, find a bathroom, navigate high-speed roads during rush hour. We never say "I'll try." Trying is far from doing. The willful-mind, plagued by the fear of failure, needs excuses and escape clauses, while the heart needs only the living present. When there is no conclusion but openness to what is, when there is nothing to accomplish but a loving regard for the moment, when honesty and heartful awareness have made our vision clear, we can see whatever the moment requires and respond appropriately.

This means we can take heart in our own, innate common sense. It always amazes me how well people find they can live and resolve even serious problems when they sit down, take a breath, get honest, stop saying "I don't know," and let their wisdom speak to them. There is no need to fear doing anything wrong. All we have to do is let go, open our awareness with honesty and compassion, relax, and receive. The sun is there, behind the cloud cover. All we need to know, we know already, or will in good time.

COMPLAINING

ONE COMMON INDICATION that we are clinging to our suffering is *complaining*, which, by the way, should not be confused with opening our heart to a friend and confiding our pain. Such trust and the releasing of emotions is healing and an essential part of recovery. Complaining, on the other hand, while it may give us a feeling of self-righteousness, involves no real trust or openness and no healing. It only keeps us stuck. The willful-mind is full of complaints about everything: the news, the weather, dinner, the way our partner leaves the cap off the toothpaste or the dresser drawers open, taxes, associates at work—the list is endless. We may even complain about God or the universe for atrocities and other events that violate our moral sensibilities. The willful-mind likes to express itself by saying "I hate———."

The most revealing and universal characteristic of complaining is its *complete ineffectiveness*. By paying attention to the process, we note that, when we complain, we frequently do so to someone who is not in a position to solve the problem. This is because the complaining mind has no use for solutions. Its sole interest is in feeling the resistance inherent in complaining because resistance strengthens the willful-mind's sense of itself. This is a subtle fact of mind-identity. The willful-mind seeks to control the world around it (which includes other people) and feels its strength in overcoming resistance. Resistance is, therefore, of utmost importance to the mind, and this is why those who are strongly identified with the mind have great difficulty letting go, admitting mistakes, or apologizing.

Complaining, then, not only denies the reality of the true self's innate effectiveness—it is also an act of fraud: The complaining mind *pretends* to care about changing whatever it complains about but actually has no such interest. The complaint serves the purpose of feeding the mind's need for resistance and control, allowing it to *believe* it cares without requiring the enthusiastic action that follows naturally from real caring. Complaining is a disguise the willful-mind puts on to keep us from recognizing that *it has no living interest in what it is complaining about.* The complaining mind is addicted to control and resists the world. It complains to hide its lack of caring behind the ready convenience of empty protest and is unwilling to take a stand in its own word, to bring to life the vision *it claims to have.* While the mind usually feels justified in its complaints, however, it eventually grows tired of being ineffective. When it has grown sufficiently tired, and if it pays careful attention to what is happening when it complains—what precedes the complaint, what happens during it, what follows—it may catch on that complaining is an acting out of the victim role. Once we are aware of this, we are unlikely to continue choosing to be the victim. Rather, our very awareness frees us from the tyranny of unexamined habit. From that point on, the things about which we feel an urge to complain may be seen as opportunities for us to find out how honest we are being, how much we really care about the thing we claim to care about, how much we have fallen out of the compassionate heart back into the willful-mind. We may then find that we stop complaining and start acting. There is no need for complaining when we are in touch with our own spontaneous enthusiasm and competence, when we are aware of who we are.

As an exercise, think of something you recently complained about, then consider what you are *willing* to do to improve the situation. If you find yourself unwilling to do anything, you will have caught the complaining mind in the act of pretending to care. Pay close attention to this unmasking; watch it without judging it. Since the problem really does not matter to you sufficiently for you to invest yourself in solving it, ask yourself what you are getting out of complaining. Feel the *superiority* hiding behind the complaining mind, how its sense of separateness is fed. Now, identify a problem about which you *are* willing to do something. Turn your attention to your heart and let yourself become aware of what you would like to do to help solve the problem. Note the sense of fulfillment that accompanies an awareness of the heart's natural expression of caring through compassionate action. When we practice lovingly letting the moment come and go, there is nothing to complain about. This love makes things workable. Those who live from the heart wake up and move into the day with enthusiasm.

NEW PAIN, OLD PAIN

As THOUGH SUMMONED by our grief over having been left, the "demons" of many past hurts, even from childhood, begin to enter our awareness. The willful-mind, constricted and resistant by nature, is ill-equipped to offer these demons the compassion they hunger for and may experience this surge of sorrow from the inner mists and shadows of the psyche as an all-out attack. Invariably, it attempts to come up with a conclusion that will allow it to feel in control and make sense of so much intense feeling. Here, as always, self-analyzing is of little value; all we end up with is the mind's conclusions, which are very far from the heart of the matter. On the other hand, we can further our recovery by simply, lovingly noting the specific details of thought, emotion, and physical sensation, for example, whether the pain is welling up in the chest or throat, how deep inside the body it reaches, any phasing or shift in intensity, any images that come to mind.

As a feeling or sensation comes, then, pay attention, take a deep breath and let it out, then pay *closer* attention. Have you felt this before, been left before? If so, examine the associated feelings. Have you been dreaming about the earlier abandonment, confusing the partners during the dream, their faces or names? Has your sadness over the present situation prompted tender or pain-ful recollections of one or the other parent? Grandparent? We have been in exile from our hearts for a lifetime. Our hurts go farther back than we realize, and often our adult partnerships play and replay many of them all at once. This is not to suggest that we ought to go on a wild goose chase through the past. Again, the willful-mind is not the vehicle of recovery, and its stories and conclusions cannot heal us. It is to point out, however, that sometimes we are not clear about what is really hurting us. We must be willing to let it all stand before us, to feel it all, to pass through countries of inner exile in order to come home. A close friend or skilled therapist can serve as your guide through these painful passages and help you admit into awareness what-ever has hurt you so it can be released. You may need to weep about many things you never took the time to feel. Life has a funny way of keeping its books. Sooner or later, emotions pushed underground find their way back to the surface and demand their due.

A loving awareness in the moment can free us from even long-standing patterns of suffering. We have hurt for so long. I have not met a person who is not carrying enormous pain in his heart. It seems almost too simple that we could begin to throw off our habit of numbness and chronic, repetitive patterns of second pain simply by practicing being present. But we owe it to ourselves to consider: All our life, when are we really fully present? When, for example, driving the car, are we simply driv-ing the car and not doing a hundred other things in our mind? Have we given the present a chance? Have we even once felt the steering wheel, how the seat both gives under our weight and supports us, the passing shapes and colors, the orderly flow of traffic, the way the heat rises up in waves from the highway, the sudden acceleration of the car in front as it races through a yellow light, and on and on, each moment, as it is, with no one in the way? This state of open awareness is described in Emer-son's *Nature:* "Standing on the bare ground . . . all mean egotism vanishes. I become a transparent eyeball; I am nothing; I see all;

the currents of the Universal Being circulate through me." Even a little time spent in this loving awareness of the present can be tremendously liberating. We begin to realize that this "I" with which we have so identified ourselves, is in fact, merely another thought in the mind! There is no separate "I." There is only this moment, this awareness of life in its course, as it is, right now, with all that presents itself, including this person being aware! The moment arises, presents itself, falls away, into the next and the next and the next.

When we have not yet made the leap "out of our mind," we may wonder how a simple, loving awareness of the present could be so joyful. Here, the mind is playing the role of a clever scholar, asking "Why?" in order to avoid surrendering to the heart. I know of no answer to this "why," any more than I know why a tree falling in the forest makes a sound. It is simply so. The Buddhists call this fundamental fact of being in its course "suchness," and associate it with the ringing of a bell, with simplicity, clarity, wholeness. Open awareness in the living present *is* joyful, without reasons; it is simply "such." And even a few moments in this suchness can begin to gently penetrate decades of armor built up around the heart.

The poet Robert Bly wrote: "Who is it we spend our entire life loving?"[1] Ultimately, is it not our heart itself that we long for, and a self that is clearer, more aware, and more alive than the self we have, in our fear, taken ourselves to be? Perhaps this is the true beloved, the very spirit of life within us, which our deepest hurts lead us to forget or deny. Somewhere along the way we lost solidarity with this self; we began to look to the world for signs of our worth, and its invalidations only addicted us all the more to looking outward. We stopped listening to our heart; abandoned it, took flight from the present into futile fantasies of separateness. We began our exile from the true garden and put on the mantle of homesickness.

[1]Robert Bly, trans., "Poem 20," *The Kabir Book: Forty-Four of the Ecstatic Poems of Kabir* (Boston: Beacon Press, 1977), p. 27.

In the face of a lifetime of such homesickness, the heart's gentle voice is drowned out for a while. Now, caught in an avalanche of pain, you may feel you are very far from being able either to hear it or to entertain such profound notions as your "real identity." But you are more than able and always have been; all that is required is that you pay loving attention to your own suffering and that this time, rather than running from it or "making it better," you go into it, heart leading. The path back to the heart we have encased in armor is a path of tears. There is no other way. As Marilyn Ferguson wrote in *The Aquarian Conspiracy*, "Our pathology is our opportunity."[2] This is not much comfort if the only opportunity you are interested in is the opportunity for reunion with your partner. The self that dwells in the living present, the heart-self, cannot guarantee that your partner will return, and you already know this. And if he or she did come back at this point, you might well lose the opportunity Ferguson refers to, for your sense of identity and well-being would again be based on an outer condition that has nothing to do with your innate capacity to enter your spacious heart and affirm your life unconditionally. Remember, your beloved is only a person, a person probably working under the influence of strongly conflicting inner forces, a person tossed between delusion and reality, between his or her own mind and heart, a person who has gone through much hurt, too. Each must make the journey to what is real. Each must establish solidary with the heart or spend life careening from circumstance to circumstance, from desire to desire, from disappointment to disappointment, all the while burying the heart deeper in denial and numbness. Sooner or later, we must turn our attention to all that is buried there. Your heart won't deceive you with empty reassurances about the future, then, but will speak lovingly and clearly to you of your own greater identity. It will comfort you and heal you from the

[2]Marilyn Ferguson, *The Aquarian Conspiracy* (Los Angeles: Houghton Mifflin, 1980), p. 25.

injuries inflicted by your long-term banishment in the world of the willful-mind. Listen to it. You will find in it the seeds of a life renewed and a way out of both old and new pain that you may not have imagined.

LOOKING BACK

FOR A WHILE after my wife left, I made the mistake of keeping wedding photographs around. My willful-mind loved it; it allowed me to feel so miserable! When someone we love leaves, we may spend a great deal of time looking back, for it seems there is nowhere else to look; there we relive good memories in order to feel sorry for ourselves and bad ones in order to feel justified in our guilt or anger. The present seems a closed door, and the future promises nothing if it does not promise reconciliation. We become obsessed with the person who has left, and for a while, perhaps, this is to be expected. Often, we romanticize the past, filling the mind with inflated assessments of the partner's good qualities and, unfortunately, an often heartless critique of ourselves, of all we did wrong and could have done—should have done—to prevent things from coming to this. There is something to be said for self-evaluation; the willingness to change, to do better, is the hallmark of a generous spirit. On the other hand, much of this inventory taking is almost certain to be lopsided, biased by the confusion resulting from the shock of sheer loss. Adults who have been left by their lovers are adults in the depths of rejection; they often assume blame where it does not belong the same way children project an image of their parents as faultless.

Self-indictment has more to do with the fear of losing control than anything else. Again, this is willful-mind at work. "If you left because of something I did, you may come back if I behave differently. If I was bad, I can be better; if I am better, you'll come back. Therefore, your coming back is under my control." This is simplistic self-deception and, in true willful-mind style, a denial of what is real: It reduces your partner's will to a function of your own, which it is not. It also absolves him or her of the responsibility for having left and probably ignores much of what went on that led to the decisive act. Reviewing the past in a way that makes only one person essentially responsible for the problems of the partnership is dehumanizing and a fantasy. Unfortunately, it can be a very powerful fantasy, reinforced by our belief in it. In such a case and regardless of our partner's contributions to the problems, we can feel convinced that the breakup was essentially our fault and that our partner left as a last resort. Such self-judgment can be almost unbearable if deeply believed and can pour fuel on the fire of helplessness and desperation.

Simply being aware of the tendency to fall into this kind of judgmental recreation of the past can protect us to some degree. There are, however, three specific points that it will help to note and take to heart:

1. Love is a collaboration. It always involves difficulties. Particularly when these difficulties become serious, both partners must be willing to work out a solution together, or the partnership simply becomes unviable. Your partner's decision to leave does not shift total responsibility to you, regardless of what you think you could or should have done. You are not solely responsible for what has happened.

2. Dwelling on all that you miss about your absent partner is an expression of the pain of helplessness; it does not accurately reflect life with

that partner. If nothing else, such prejudiced remembering leaves out or greatly plays down the conflicts that preceded and led up to the separation. *Especially if these recollections intensify feelings of desperation,* do not give them significance. Recognize them for what they are: mind-dramas in which we make our own will the deciding factor ("I caused all of this") in order to indulge in the fantasy that we can now cause our partner to return by an act of will ("I'll change").

3. Remember some of the bad, too. This is not to blame your partner. Remembering the bad is a balancing exercise, not a decision against reconciliation. It will, however, help keep you out of the trap of assuming excessive responsibility for any problems the two of you had.

Your greatest ally when you find yourself caught up in painful self-recrimination is to bring a loving awareness to the living present. Note what is going on within you, without identifying with it: "Painful memory of being together in the theater . . . A feeling of missing her . . . Tears coming . . . An ache in the throat. . . ." As your awareness opens and the constrictions around the heart relax, you will find there is more than enough room for these moments to arise, express themselves, and fall away. The sadness will be there, the memories, the longing; that may not be different. But you will discover something new and amazing: *As you develop the reunion with your own heart, you will find the pain of separation from your former partner lessening.* In its place will be a love that transcends conditions of physical and even emotional separateness because it transcends the willful-mind. This love is the love within which we can never lose those we love, within which we can offer our love to them each day because our love is no longer one that looks for favors to be returned, no longer a love we "give and take," as though it were a business. It is a love we have become, the beginning of an entirely new identity. By releasing resistance to our sorrow, we find ample room within us for all feelings to come and go in the present, and in the present we experience a joy that can never be found in what was or will be. We find we are neither looking back nor waiting for the future to take our pain away from us. By entering the generosity and kindness of our own heart, we no longer need to *suffer* our pain. Within the miracle of the living present, we discover a compassion that allows us to look back and let go of looking back in the same moment.

REUNION

THE WILLFUL-MIND does not like to hear that the way out of suffering has nothing to do with reunion or any other circumstance but depends on a shift in awareness one has to make alone by moving from delusion to reality, from self-escape to self-affirmation, from addiction to a deep letting-go, from reaction to a life of simple, open awareness in the here and now. Seeing this is a matter of detaching oneself from the desperation long enough to gain a sense of oneself as the calm, gentle watcher. *Desperation for reunion is a measure of how little reunion would make a difference.* For similar reasons, actors have a saying: "Never go to an audition hungry." They know about second pain, that the fear of fear creates fear. In the same manner, desperation for reunion at best creates a desperate reunion, and that is certainly not likely to go well. It may seem unfair that the more desperate we feel the need for something, the less likely we are to get it, but, fair or not, this is often the way human stories play themselves out. In this sense, our partner's leaving may actually provide us with the opportunity to come face to face with our own self-exile, to the extent that we are willing to take an honest look at the desperation we call love. *Desperation is characteristic of addiction, not love.* Of course, when we have been abandoned, we feel great pain, confusion, a sense of having been betrayed. None of this, however, necessarily involves feelings of desperation, that horrible sense that "I *must* have my partner back or life is simply not bearable." Desperation is denial with the gloves off, an all-out clutching at images that reality refuses to support. This is the willful-mind at its worst, creating a deep, inner separateness. Partners lost in this inner separateness, who have not come home to the wholeness of their heart and entered into an acceptance of the living present as it is, beyond their control and desires, will not be able to find a way to be together, regardless of their living arrangements.

The central issue, then, is not reunion, but rather our becoming aware of what is really happening within us. "Know thyself," pronounced the ancient Greek oracle, and with those two words, the whole of Western philosophy began. Without this self-knowledge or, better, self-clarity, delusions run rampant and desperation rules the day. Strategic thinking, second guessing, complaints, and compromised negotiating do not bring us what we want; they only serve to distract us from heart-awareness, which is the real remedy for the desperation of thwarted desire. The best thing we can do in the face of having been left is stop, look, and listen: stop the immediate urge to react in desperation, look at the situation to see what is really taking place, and listen to our heart.

It is natural for the willful-mind to be fairly obsessed with thoughts of reunion, and particularly with how to bring that about. Ironically, even reunion is more likely to occur within the ease of a deep letting-go, as a by-product of loving regard for our predicament and a refusal to identify with desperation, but we must be careful here, lest this idea itself be misconstrued as a strategy: "If I just relax and let go, my partner will come back." Such ploys, no matter how subtle, are self-defeating and only tighten the coils of suffering around us. Better, then, to put the question of reunion aside and deal with the essential matter at hand. Sooner or later, we must be willing to see things as they are and let them come to us or not on their own terms. This is far from the "make it happen" battle-cry of the Western hero who pits his will against nature, cuts down every obstacle, and emerges victorious (usually just before the credits roll). But this sort of hard determination has repercussions, and to the extent that we oppose life this way, it opposes us as well. We may either prevail over the world or belong to it, but not both. We may either indict or forgive our partner, but not both. We may either live our life within the adversarial terms of the willful-mind or enter into our true identity and *become* that love that is alone truly unconditional. If we choose to open ourselves to the living present in kind awareness and forgiveness, we find we are in love with a squirrel who bravely ventures close to take a crust of bread as much as we are in love with our partner, in love with the soft light of the predawn hours as much as we are in love with our children. But we cannot have it both ways. "No man can serve two masters," taught Jesus. Nor can we postpone forever this central question of who is living our life, the question of our identity. If we do not allow ourselves to enter the present, to admit our fear and pain and grief so we may finally stop running from them, if we do not open our awareness and choose the heart as our master, life will bring us to a point where we will have to face the fact that we chose by failing to choose. How much longer will we defer our own heart, which is aching for our recognition? Will we wait our whole life, until, on our death bed, with unspeakable regret and loved ones standing around helpless, we realize we have never lived? In his *Confessions,* Augustine wrote: "Too late I loved you, O Beauty ever ancient and ever new! Too late I loved you! And, behold, you were within me, and I out of myself, and there I searched for you." We do not need to postpone the joy that is given to us. We do not need to continue suffering. Now is the perfect time to begin to allow the transformation from mind-identity to heart-identity to take place. Joy is present. Wholeness and recovery are present. It is we, lost in the desert of our desires and denials, who are not present. *And it is our return, not our partner's that is needed.* Here, we come upon an understanding that may be as startling in principle as it is liberating in practice:

Love does not depend on outer circumstances. It is possible for us to affirm our love even for one who has left us.

Someone may deny us intimacy, closeness, access, even contact, but this is in no way requires us to deny the love we have in our heart for that person. Nor—and it is important to add this here—does our continuing to love someone who has chosen to leave us mean we cannot go on with our life, perhaps to discover a richer, healthier, more wholehearted love with someone else. The point is that our love for another can be with us as a genuine, active, and valued part of our experience even if the person we so love is no longer physically present. Despite the willful-mind's conviction that "love" entitles us to possess and control another, the heart understands that love is not exclusive and does not view the beloved solely in terms of desire. Our vision is so limited; we do not know what path another may need to take, and never is our love greater than in the willingness to let the beloved go on, if that is required.

Centered in the heart, we begin to realize and celebrate the fact that everyone we have ever loved is part of us, and we of them. These bridges, once built, continue in the form of influences we may hardly appreciate. How different would we be if we had not met even one person we have loved? Do we not sometimes hear ourselves laughing at a joke as our beloved might have? Do we not on occasion have a thought or insight that we sense comes directly from all we learned in the time we shared with him or her? It is not love that makes separation unbearable; it is the willful-mind's need to possess and control love. And this is torture because love cannot be possessed, controlled. Consequently, as long as we are identified with the willful-mind, we must fear the very love we profess to seek. The willful-mind must always subvert what it cannot control, and it is not surprising that many of us have had the experience of undermining love relationships, sabotaging them precisely when things seemed to be going best.

As the mind's habitual authority yields to the openness of the heart, we begin to realize that our love for another frees us from the need to possess him or her, even in the form of an active relationship. We can let the beloved go on, and we can go on as well. Those we have loved and who have loved us are part of us. We will always feel the warmth of those precious things about them that continue to live in us, no matter how many years or miles may come between. When we are quiet, gently aware in the living present, and turn our attention to anyone with whom we have been in love, we can feel a deep interest in their well-being and a stirring gratitude for our having known and loved them, for our knowing and loving them still in every way that matters. When we come home to our heart, all those we love are there with us. In such a fullness, physical distance becomes a nearly irrelevant detail. The real reunion takes place in the heart of each of us.

RECOVERY

In the difficult are the friendly forces, the hands
that work on us.

—RAINER MARIA RILKE
Letters

COCOONING AND BUTTERFLYING

ONE OF THE MOST STRIKING EXAMPLES of change is the metamorphosis of a caterpillar into a butterfly. Before its transformation, the creature is earthbound, slow, colorless, and confined within the darkness of its tiny, spun chamber; afterward, it is light, airborne, quick, radiant with color, a miracle brought about by time and the biological guidance provided within the natural order. Such is the power of the present moment to transform. Though the larva works tirelessly to build and later escape its cocoon, we recognize that it is merely following its nature, and, therein, its effort is effortless. It does not seem to need to figure out how to work the magic of metamorphosis. Poetically, perhaps, it "follows its heart," but we suspect that it can do no other. We humans, on the other hand, have a hard time with transformation. We are impatient, loath to trust what we cannot see with our eyes. The resistance inherent in our having identified with the willful-mind sets us apart from the larger reality of wholeness in which we, as heart-selves, can participate. As long as we are stuck in this resistance, in suffering, we cannot cooperate with the natural forces of transition. We either deny and resist change or try to force it. We attempt to get to the butterfly by ripping open the cocoon; we pry open the rosebud to reach the blossom, forgetting that the timing of things is inseparable from the things themselves. Compelled by the willful-mind's impatience, intent on the gratification of the desires we mistakenly believe will fulfill us, we run roughshod over the world and each other, oblivious to the present, asleep to the delight and humor of being.

Every life is a story with inevitable times of transition, and we deny ourselves much of our humanness when we resist these times, when we struggle prematurely in the cocoons of our transformation. On the path of recovery, we see this again and again. Perhaps we struggle against the end of a relationship in which our former partner, for whatever reasons, is no longer interested. Or we struggle to keep our grief at bay, to avoid fully embracing whatever within us has been needing our embrace all our life. As our awareness opens, we may even find ourselves struggling to stay in our heart, which is something like trying to be spontaneous. But as the shift to the heart-center proceeds, we find we can more and more readily recognize when effort is premature, misguided, or of no avail. At such times, we are in the cocoons of transition and have the great opportunity to practice letting-go.

Letting-go means not resisting the forces at work in and around us. It means *doing nothing,* refraining from habits of control and misplaced effort and deferring to the healing process as something inherently natural and assured. "Do nothing, everything will be done," says the *Tao-te Ching.* Though an offense to Western thinking, which considers such a suggestion an invitation to idleness and failure, this statement is subtle in its wisdom. Change is inevitable, ongoing. Rather than succumbing to our impatience and attempting to force a situation, thereby undermining the natural timing of things and defeating ourselves, we can step back from it, watch it, and remember that, contrary to appearances, it is already changing. By calling upon the natural clarity and patience of simple awareness, we find we are able to recognize the time to act, and to act without being heavy-handed or intrusive. Letting-go does not mean we do not participate. It means we participate through alertness and cooperation, with a light touch.

When the days seem either too empty or too filled with painful memories, you may feel that, if you don't do something, you'll go out of your mind. This is precisely where you need to go, since it is the willfulness of the mind, and not the situation we are in, that perpetuates suffering. Remember, there is nothing to do. No singles bars to visit halfheartedly, no need to agree to blind dates set up by well-meaning friends, no judgment that ten thousand tears are enough to have shed and "best get on with it." Practice doing nothing but opening the heart and being aware, in detail, of what is before you. Do not attempt to fill time prematurely with activity or force positive moods on yourself; nor do you need to spend time stewing or being negative. Recovery is a balancing act. And if it feels like an act for a while, open your heart to that, too. All you need to do is remember that healing is inherent. You are human, you have been injured, and you are healing. Your body breathes, it circulates blood, it transmutes food into cells and carries out thousands of vital functions and activities each moment, all without your "doing" anything! Such is the effectiveness of letting-go. Trust your being, then; it has not abandoned you. Let the sleepless nights be sleepless. Fly on "automatic" if you need to, and, in general, do the best you can. There is peace in this willingness. Follow, don't try to lead. Take slow, deep breaths when the pain is at its worst, accepting it into your heart so you can embrace it and offer your compassion to yourself just as you would offer it to another in pain. Sigh. Let go. Trust.

GIVING AND RECEIVING

A BROKEN HEART is an immeasurably valuable opportunity. In fact, there may be no better way for our heart to become open to its own spaciousness than by being broken open. Paying attention to the sense of desperation that claws at the solar plexis, the aching emptiness that wells up in the chest and throat, the weighty despondency that draws the head down, the electricity in the arms and hands that has nowhere to go because there is no longer anything to be done to bring the beloved back—all of this shows us we are going through the same sort of withdrawal people go through when they stop taking daily doses of heroin or alcohol. As the willful-mind is dethroned by its own helplessness in the face of loss, it releases its clutching and we begin to see that our suffering is a statement, not about our situation but about our relation to pain itself. We have not yet learned how to move gracefully through pain. We panic, fight it, deny it, judge it, hate it. And the more we struggle against our pain, the more we are drawn into it like quicksand, the more we practice being closed to our own heart in a way that makes living difficult and healing impossible.

We are imprisoned in misplaced identification with thinking, doing, winning, with having things "our way." We are impris-

oned in our addiction to conclusions, knowing, impatience, pre-
occupations with the past and the future that squander the precious present. We are imprisoned in the need to control so many
things that are beyond our control, especially love, which, by
nature, cannot be controlled. We are imprisoned in countless
fears and unexpressed grief over all we have lost and all we know
we must lose, over the numberless moments we were not fully
present, not fully alive. We are imprisoned in measuring our
worth through the opinions and actions of others rather than
directly, through a cultivated awareness of the miracle that we
are alive at all. We are imprisoned in a practiced unwillingness
to surrender to the simple joy of the living present, without
conditions and demands. We are imprisoned in the pattern of
continually engineering our own disappointment. We are imprisoned in the habit of taking the miraculous completely for
granted—our own breathing, for example—while assigning
great status to the mind's false gods, such as being right. And
what can we do having little or no awareness of our inherent
lovableness and worth, living within armor that makes it nearly
impossible for us to feel that we are alive? When our heart is
broken, however, we may for the first time look in the mirror and
see reflected the face of our own incarceration. In such a moment
the will to live may be sparked in a new, wholehearted way.

I remember an occasion when, clearly seeing how closed I had
been, I suddenly felt less troubled by the fact that one day I
would die than by the fact that I might die never having lived.
With great sadness, I realized I had spent very little time in the
present, simply giving what was asked of me and accepting what
I wished to accept of what was offered. I sensed for the first time
that I had been hiding far away in myself, locked in a dream of
desire, control, unreality. To the willful-mind, with which I had
so identified, giving had become largely associated with a sense
of obligation, and, deep within me, receiving felt like stealing. At
the center of this surprising insight was another: I neither gave
nor received wholeheartedly because I was terrified of making
mistakes, of failing, of not being good enough. "I will not be part

of this life I see around me; it cannot be trusted," I concluded, and, as a result of believing this, I dared not risk emotional participation. Within this tacit commitment to stay an outsider, giving and receiving would have to feel fraudulent, a mere going through the motions. I had become a person who lived in a world that could not be trusted, an imposing, dangerous world where neither giving nor receiving retained their natural, spontaneous goodness. In such a world, relinquishing control and joyfully taking part were out of the question.

When we are unwilling to live in the openness of the heart, we are like a closed hand, which can neither give nor receive. We move through life like a fist—constricted, self-wearying, angry, quick to take offense, ready to lash out. A fist cannot offer, cannot support, cannot sustain, cannot feel, cannot express anything but its own hardness. When we accept the present, however, relinquishing criticism and conclusions and simply being with whatever is before us, we find the fist relaxing, the hand opening. Giving and receiving can proceed naturally; we are free to give what is ours to give and receive that which is offered to us as we may wish. At home in both giving and receiving, we no longer need an agenda of winning, taking, outsmarting, of always having to push ourselves toward the next fantasy. All this strategy is replaced by the charm of the moment, which, it might be said, is always giving something and asking us to give something in return. The moment may give the tranquility of twilight and the soothing music of migrating birds against a slate sky, asking in return that we not let such a moment go unnoticed, unappreciated. It may give us the deep aching that comes when we remember how our former partner buttoned a shirt or the way the house smelled when she took fresh cookies from the oven and placed them on a newspapered kitchen counter, asking in return that we love this one memory of our partner's sweetness for what it is without having to possess it, that we let our love deepen despite our sadness, perhaps even because of it. Missing someone we love has its loveliness, after all. Giving and receiving are part of life lived from the heart; there is no ownership there, no possessing, no clinging. In this sense, giving and receiving are the natural ebb and flow of letting-go and being fully alive. Whether the moment brings happy or sad memories, we can remain wholeheartedly present in it. We can give and receive without comparing, judging, regretting, without urgency or crisis, without having to do anything at all. We can remain open, even when the mind prompts us to go chasing after the good memories and fills us with anger or remorse over the bad ones. We can let life flow to and from us in the natural dialogue of giving and receiving that contributes so greatly to our healing.

NATURAL FORGIVENESS

ONE REASON we feel so violated by abandonment is that we sense that love is supposed to last forever. "I thought I knew him, but he changed. I guess I only thought he loved me." "We were so close, I can't figure it out." "How can you trust anybody after something like this?" These and similar vexations are common during and immediately after abandonment. They express the most pervasive emotional shock. How is it possible that one so loved and trusted is now a stranger, is now not only unworthy of trust, but emotionally dangerous? The willful-mind grows dizzy racing for explanations. If, as Shakespeare wrote, "Love alters not with his [Time's] brief hours and weeks, / But bears it out, even to the edge of doom," how are we to understand a love that is no more? Either love is temporary after all, merely the product of changing circumstances or—and this is perhaps the worse explanation—we were deceived all along. Love is forever, so this could not have been love. Perhaps it was a pretense of love, a relationship based on favors exchanged, on security, on something else, but not "real" love, which grows and adjusts and finds ways to endure.

This doubt can be excruciating. Caught in its turbulence, we may feel a million miles from any sort of peace. In shock, we struggle to understand any sense in which it is still possible to believe in love, perhaps even still believe in this love, despite our partner's having left. Hanging by a thread of faith and hope, we find ourselves faced with a terrible choice: to believe love abides and that, therefore, this love was no love, or to believe that love vanishes. It is Sophie's choice.[1] It seems we must give up either our faith in a lifelong love or our faith in our ability to recognize it.

Behind this reasoning we can detect the black-or-white, judgmental thinking that characterizes the willful-mind, and we may find some comfort in recognizing that human life is an evolving process that is seldom black or white. As we get older, we have the opportunity to grow a little wiser, a little less demanding, a little more openhearted and aware of what is real. We can appreciate that while a healthy, mature love could certainly last a lifetime, there are varying degrees of health and maturity, and love can only be as healthy and mature as those who have entered into it. Your partner's leaving does not mean that he or she did not love you. It may mean that he or she was not able to love you particularly well. Like so many of us, your absent partner is probably under the influence of the delusions, denials, and addictions of the willful-mind. These make a mature, evolving love, one generous enough to sustain itself in the living present, all but out of the question. Still, as your compassion for your own predicament grows, you will come to realize your partner loved you as best he or she could. We are all on the way to a greater capacity for love and heart-awareness, and the journey is not easy for any of us. Have we not have all, at times, fallen short of the mark, and isn't this precisely the "human predicament": to awaken from the mind's dream-spinning to what is real and embrace the life that is given to us here, now, even as we sit reading?

Before recovery "took hold" in my awareness, I was particularly unforgiving toward anyone who, professing love, commit-

---

[1] From William Styron's chilling tale *Sophie's Choice*, in which a woman is forced to choose which of her two small children she will turn over to the Nazis for extermination.

ted deeply unloving acts and blamed them on circumstances. My mind, skilled in keeping me far from my heart, reasoned thus: "Love is a commitment that makes itself known in actions, not words. Circumstances are irrelevant. What sense does it make to say 'I love you,' if I then break your heart? What sense does it make to believe that the child-abusing mother loves her little one when she fractures his leg in a fit of mindless rage?" As my heart opened a little, however, I discovered a different voice. This is what it said: "While love is a great determiner of action, circumstances also have their place, and the loving heart appreciates this, allows this most of all. *The broken heart is a preface to an open heart,* to a majestic mountain range of forgiveness, wonderful to behold on the inner landscape. It sounds the depth and breadth of the soul. From its heights, you already know the child abuser does often love the child but so hates himself that rage is finally the only outlet. It is not to excuse, but to understand. Such a one is in agony and has no idea in the world of where to turn."

As anger subsides and heart-awareness opens, we begin to realize that our former partner did not do anything to us at all. We rarely understand the reality of another, involving as it does a complex balance of forces reaching far beyond the context of our own pain. It is quite a day when we are able to appreciate this and begin to work with our own reality, which is the only thing we can or need to do to attain a measure of peace and gladness in being alive.

The great Sufi, Pir Hazrat Inayat Khan, said "You must let your heart break entirely, otherwise there will be bitterness." At a certain point in our recovery, as we continue to melt the armor around our heart, we are ready to enter into the possibility of forgiveness. The willful-mind despises forgiveness because forgiveness dissolves boundaries and resistances, but the heart knows there is much, both in ourselves and others, that needs to be forgiven and thereby released. Our own real suffering reveals to us the reality of the suffering of others, including those who, numbed by years of delusion, guilt, and self-hatred, caused us pain. We begin to see the truth of the universality of suffering, proclaimed by the Buddha five hundred years before Christ. In our world, each day, so many are hungry for food. But aren't we all hungry for a kind word, a little appreciation, a moment of feeling—even if only in some slight way—heroic and valuable? Opening our heart, we realize that, for the most part, we do not intend to be cruel, to inflict pain on others, but that we live in a confusing time and have lost our way. We do the best we can, all things considered, and often it is not very good. Plato said no one knowingly does what is wrong and that when others inflict suffering on us, they cannot, at that moment, help it. This is no bleeding-heart acceptance of irresponsibility, but rather a recognition that, even in the most horrible acts, there is a prior horror from which the act springs. For good or ill, we pass on what we were given, and the mind is faithful to these inheritances far more than we know. As heart-awareness deepens, the mind's black-or-white judgments dissolve into the many grays of compassion. The heart, while not excusing hurtful acts, recognizes and accepts, with great sadness, their origin in the inevitable, intergenerational contagion of human suffering. Inherently generous, the heart understands the injury and subsequent numbness that precipitate these acts and chooses to offer the balm of forgiveness rather than inflict further injury through blame and retaliation, which the willful-mind justifies under the banner of "principle." Love is not a principle, nor is it black or white. It understands the gray areas, the humanness of humans, the role of circumstances, and allows for retrograde motion, mistakes, times of transition. It does not feel compelled, when something goes wrong, to hurl accusations and blame. While some may consider this a maudlin denial of the offending act, it is the basis of real forgiveness, and it is the heart's natural way. Jesus demonstrated this when he prayed, "Father, forgive them; for they know not what they do." We are all sleepwalking to a degree, thrashing about in our private reality, running into and, in some cases, over each other. The basis of suffering in human life, then, is not cruelty but unconsciousness, a lack of heart. *And we cannot, no matter how much we may wish to, open the heart of another.* That is a personal matter subject to its own timing. It is finally the responsibility and right of each of us to begin a program of recovery so that we can open our own heart to the joyful miracle of being alive, of being human and humanly conscious in a world where things change and loss is inevitable.

As compassion for ourselves and our predicament deepens, forgiveness enters the picture, not as moral license extended to one who hurt us, but as the only salve that can soothe our broken heart. We see that forgiveness is a matter of honestly acknowledging the offense inflicted without automatically *assuming the right* to condemn the offending party. Who can say, after all, what delusional forces another is laboring under? Who can stop to consider the possible agony in the soul of the one who causes the pain? There is a remarkable saying: "Everything in the world is either an act of love or a cry for love." If we could see "through the eyes of eternity," we might realize there is no one to forgive but ourselves for the quickness with which we, blind to another's suffering, convicted him solely on the basis of our own. Kahlil Gibran, in his great work *The Prophet,* asks: "How shall you punish those whose remorse is already greater than their misdeeds?" Forgiveness is not a matter of moral duty, which at best fosters in us a sense of superiority, thereby separating us from each other and our own heart even more. Rather, it is a spontaneous outpouring of love, and love always unites. The self that can forgive is the self that is lovingly, compassionately aware of its own suffering and so can recognize the suffering of others and extend compassion naturally toward them. What we give to ourselves we can give to others. True forgiveness reveals and affirms our fundamental sameness. In its light, both the "perpetrator" and the "victim" of the offense are embraced by the awareness that there is so much more to who we are than even the most spellbinding of the dramatic roles with which we identify. As long as we feel we cannot forgive or believe we should forgive as a moral obligation, to be nice, and so on, we are not yet centered in our heart.

Natural forgiveness flows from a merciful awareness of the pain *we* are in. This is not self-pity: indeed, such a term prompts us to ask, "Which self?" The mind loves self-pity. Perhaps this is what Herman Hesse meant when he wrote, "Depression is arrogance."[2] The heart does not pity. It simply loves, embraces, takes unto itself, makes room for. It has a light touch, the light touch of patience, attentiveness to detail, gratitude, humor, forgiveness. As the delightful saying goes: "Angels can fly because they take themselves lightly." It should be apparent that we cannot melt the armor surrounding the heart and reach a state of forgiveness as long as we feel this is something we *should* do—the word itself is hard, almost scolding and it is one the mind's favorites. By simply giving merciful attention to our predicament, exactly as it is, without trying to change any of it, we see that it begins to change by itself. The heaviness of the willful-mind's armor—crisis, betrayal, loneliness, grief, anger—yields to the lightness of the heart—unjudgmental awareness, trust, communion, empathy, joy, forgiveness. We need not contrive any of it. If we are feeling unforgiving, then, we need not pretend otherwise; we need only forgive our unforgiveness. It is all so human. As the heart opens, we come to a point not unlike the top of a mountain. From there, we survey all those we loved and lost, all those we hurt and who hurt us, all the younger selves we have been through our life, selves that did the best they could in their time. And from that higher perspective, forgiveness flows from us as from a fountain. We realize that all are suffering, all are aching for release from fear and guilt, for a place spacious enough to put down the burden of grief carried through a lifetime. Gradually, as we become ready, our own heart shows us there is no one to forgive, not even ourselves. Here are some things you can do to cultivate natural forgiveness:

[2]Herman Hesse, *Steppenwolf.*

Explore placing greater value on being at peace than on being right.

"Twelve-Step" programs, such as Al-Anon, which cultivate freedom from reacting addictively, employ the slogan, "How important is it?" Along these same lines, there is a story about a young soldier who happened upon the Buddha when he was deep in meditation. For fun, the soldier decided to taunt the Enlightened One, to see if he could distract him from his practice and began calling him names. An hour went by with no reaction from the Buddha. Frustrated, the soldier began cursing at the sage, who, of course, remained peacefully concentrated within. Hours passed; the sun set, and over and over, the willful soldier tried everything he could think of to threaten, to intimidate, to provoke. Into the night, he shook his fists, bellowed insults, stamped his feet, and threw himself again and again at the meditating Buddha, all to no avail. Finally, when the first traces of sun lit the horizon and the soldier lay on the ground, exhausted and defeated, the Buddha opened his eyes. "It isn't possible," said the soldier, "for anyone to remain so calm in the face of such an attack." The Buddha regarded the young man mercifully: "If someone offers you a gift and you do not accept it," he said softly, "who is left with the gift?" As the story illustrates, we are free to choose, in a situation of offense, to "refuse the gift." In this light, an offense may be viewed as an opportunity to let go rather than let loose. Admittedly, this represents a radical departure from the habit of "combat readiness" so many of us seem to have acquired and practiced most of our life. But we need only look at the face of someone caught in the vise-grip of unforgiveness to realize that the arrows of angry judgment or blame do not inflict suffering on the intended victim, but on the archer himself: The brow is furrowed, the teeth are clenched, the musculature of the face is drawn downward, the entire body is tense. And for what? Did someone call us a name? Or question the authority we imagine we must have? Perhaps someone, in a hurry for reasons we will never know or appreciate, cut us off on the highway. Or a fellow worker, put on edge by a difficult day, was curt with us. We can ask ourselves at any point, "How important is it?" We can short-circuit suffering by holding to serenity rather than sacrificing it for such trifles as being right or getting in the last word. We can refuse the "gift" of offense in order to safeguard the priceless treasure of our peace of mind. In the rare ability to do this, suffering defers to sanity.

In dealing with others, pretend that today is either the last day of your life or the last day of theirs.

Perspective is a remarkable thing. Many issues we take up with a vengeance would hold no importance for us if we knew this day would be our last. We would simply choose not to ascribe significance to them; no doubt it would take a great deal to upset such resolute serenity. We would want our day to be filled with appreciation, love, understanding, perhaps to "finish off business" and resolve conflicts, not set new ones into motion. We would choose to be generous, in our final, precious hours, with our forgiveness, our wisdom, our compassion, having no desire to waste them in pettiness or idle argument. How much difference it would make to live each day as though it were that important! This thought is not intended to arouse a sense of anxiety or morbidity, but rather to evoke a sense of earnestness. How much we take for granted! For all we know, today may *be* our last. If we honored it in this way, could we fail to cherish it? And if it proves not to be our last, but in this cherishing we discover a richness of being to which we had previously been asleep, will not the experiment have served its purpose? Natural forgiveness results spontaneously when we live life willingly and wholeheartedly.

NATURAL PATIENCE

THE WORD "PATIENCE" originally meant "to suffer," and there is something in this. When we think of being patient, we usually imagine sitting diligently, charitably, waiting for something to happen while we steadfastly refuse to get ruffled. As long as we are waiting for something to happen, however, it is only a matter of time until we suffer, until our patience turns into impatience, disappointment, frustration, and eventually, despair. There is no peace in "patience" of this sort, as when we sit "patiently" waiting for the phone to ring. To live waiting for anything is to miss the living present and therefore to miss the only life we have. We are taught early that patience is a virtue, but like all "virtues" imposed on us, it is of no value in guiding us to the spontaneous joy of living life from the heart.

There is a different kind of patience, however, that has nothing to do either with suffering or with waiting for something to happen. This patience arises naturally when we recognize and accept that even our most urgent hurts, fears, and desires, if left to their course, rise and fall away, and that life is an ongoing process whose outcomes are largely beyond our limited vision at any given time. Natural patience is found when we regard the present moment—just what is happening within and around us right now—as enough. We place our attention on the details at hand, watching the pot without anticipating when it will boil. This patience means sitting in traffic behind a stalled car and noting our frustration without judging it or identifying with it; letting go of someone we love because, right or wrong, letting go is what is being asked of us at this time; simply being with the reality at hand with the light touch of an honest, loving awareness. When we are aware, when we remain true to the present in this way, we find we can live without conclusions. We learn to practice cooperation and nonresistance in the face of that which is beyond our immediate control even when it is inconsistent with our desires. Placing our attention on the spaciousness of our own heart, on the charm of the ever-unique, present moment, we find patience in abundance. One step forward into the future of what might be, or the past of what might have been, and we are once again over our head in suffering.

The willful-mind's habit is to endlessly compare, control, jump to conclusions and attempt to enforce them. It does not wish to acknowledge that, because life is changing from moment to moment and we are subject to a larger timing of things, there is much we don't know and therefore can't control. When we shift our identity from mind to heart, our not knowing does not matter anymore because we find we can be present with what is, without conclusions, and in this ability to be present, we heal, pass beyond separateness into the unbroken wholeness of loving perception. In pitting ourselves against life and the timing of things, on the other hand, we only deepen our sense of separation, conflict, and hopelessness. The mind's insistence on knowing blocks the flow of life around and through us; we become lost to the present, frustrated, cut off from our natural belonging to the moment. Ultimately, the pain of having been left by someone we love is the same pain of separation we have always known, both in and out of love with another: the pain of all the times we were not present, were not able to be in our heart when we stood face to face with those we love, the times we could not feel, could not connect, could not see or understand or recognize and empathize with another. We cannot ease this pain of separation through attempts to contrive our own, separate happiness, nor by separating ourselves from our feelings, however painful, by condemning or avoiding them. We cannot release the constriction we feel in the throat when we remember these lost moments by heaping further judgments on our head. Only by embracing what we see in us when we pay quiet, loving attention from the heart, only by looking upon ourselves exactly as we are now, with kind eyes and forgiveness, can we begin to gain access to that roominess within us that makes real patience possible.

Impatience, more than anything else, exposes our imprisonment in the willful-mind. As long as we believe our happiness will come to us from anywhere but through identifying increasingly with our own open heart, we are condemned to eventual disappointment. Impatience is actually a form of self-cruelty, a process of interference and mistrust in which we lose the simple awareness of now in the urgency of what we want. Ironically, it is not uncommon that when we get what we imagine will make us happy, we are no happier than we were when we didn't have it. This is partly because the reality of something is rarely what we imagine it will be and partly because, if we do not practice being present when what we desire is not at hand, we will find that when it is, we can only meet it from within our practice of not being present. The person who can't find the preciousness of the moment of life without a partner—let me go a step further—who cannot find the preciousness of this very moment of heartache—is not likely to find it when the beloved returns or another happens along. The willful-mind's natural discontent cannot be satisfied by a partner, or by anything in the world, for that matter, and what many people call happiness seems often to be a lull between those crises in which the long-standing emptiness of the heart makes itself felt.

Natural patience blossoms with an awakening into the spacious present in which we lovingly make room for ourselves as we are now as distinct from our plans, desires, hopes, fears. The patience inherent in the heart naturally manifests itself in the gentleness of allowing rather than forcing, of accepting rather than resisting, of following rather than dictating and demanding, of living without conclusions, with eyes open watchfully, lovingly, to now. By finding this love within ourselves, the acceptance of who we are in this very moment, including our suffering and disappointment, by making room in our heart to accept and affirm and love all of it, we make ourselves ready to accept and affirm and love the next present, and the next, and the next. When we are simply, heartfully in the present, we find we are already patient. We can trust. We can live. Our heart is so spacious, it can admit even our pain and whisper to it, "Yes, I see, there is great disappointment here, a deep hurt; I take you in as my own child. I make room for you here. I open to you in kindness and acknowledge you in the living present. I love you." We open our heart to ourselves in this way and are heartened and healed.

Here it is important to note that natural patience is not the same as passivity. Indeed, passivity belongs more to the domain of waiting for things to happen, and natural patience, as stated, has nothing to do with waiting. When we are naturally patient, we are at home in the present, not racing off in our imagination to some desired future. We watch, but we do not merely watch— we watch in order to *see what is there;* we listen to our heart in order to *hear what is there;* we open ourselves in order to *receive and respond to what is there.* All of this we do with the understanding that, regardless of circumstances, what we want most is to reclaim our sense of being fully, joyfully alive and that this cannot be contrived by a direct act of will because being fully, joyfully alive means living in loving relation to life as something greater than our will. We can only enter this relation to greater life by *making ourselves available to it.* As it turns out, this occurs quite naturally, almost by itself, like our breathing, without conscious effort on our part, but our cooperation, our active willingness to refrain from interfering is required. We can cultivate this state of active willingness, or alert receptivity, by adopting a new attitude toward our experience—an attitude of at least experimental trust. Rather than constantly premeditating action, we can turn our attention to the miracle of the living present as it is, without any doing on our part, and at the same time trust that when and if action on our part is needed, our very alertness, readiness, and openness will allow us to recognize what action is appropriate and when to take it. Here, then, we can state an important general rule about recovery:

> *The patience, letting go, witnessing, and surrender of willfulness essential to recovery are not passive. They are all characterized by alertness, involvement, and an active readiness to receive and follow.*

As we practice this spirit of alertness, we begin to embody natural patience; we find ourselves living more meditatively and less premeditatively, though again living meditatively does not mean sitting cross-legged in a mountain cave. The word "meditative" comes from the Greek *mèdesthai*, meaning "to care for." Far from passive, this verb "care" connotes loving activity, the heart's natural expression in the world. Living meditatively means taking care of our life, which we can only do in the present since this is the only time we are ever alive.

Cultivating natural patience can be especially difficult for the brokenhearted because, when we are in the quicksand of rejection, we can find ourselves so distracted that it feels almost impossible to be present: to take the clothes out of the dryer, feel their warmth, smell their freshness, notice the familiar ways we fold them, the weight of our body against the floor, the working of muscles, just each moment as it is, in the simple minuteness of the miraculous here and now. We see that our attempts to stay within the moment are just that—attempts, and attempts that continually fail as our mind races away again and again into images that feed and amplify our suffering—memories of folding laundry with our former partner, and so on. When this happens, as it will, there is nothing for us to do but gently bring our attention back to our heart and take our very distraction into that spacious awareness, without resistance, acknowledging it as part of the living present, too. Without resistance, there are no distractions from healing. Everything becomes a way to move deeper into the heart's openness. We continue to simply note what is: stacking the folded clothes, the steps across the carpet to the linen closet, the ringing of the phone, the question of who is calling, and so on. Not analyzing, but simply being with, always attentive to now, always turning to the heart to take in whatever is present. When we find ourselves in pain, then, we simply note the pain without conclusions, extending compassion to ourselves, without racing to analyze, suppress, or otherwise escape it. Pain is a powerful tool for calling up the heart's natural healing forces. Natural patience means lovingly living in the here and now and continuing to stay in the openness of the heart so that we can accommodate whatever presents itself. Noting, focusing on the spaciousness of the heart, regarding this moment, going no farther than this, letting now be enough, not trying to figure out where it is all going or when it will get there. It is going nowhere but here, no time but now. In this way, slowly, we begin to embody a deep, natural patience that *is* recovery. As long as we fail to practice the natural patience of this heartful awareness, no situation will be able to please us for long, and we will continue running around the world in search of conclusions that the willful-mind has convinced us can fill the emptiness we feel inside, which is in fact our longing for ourselves. Nothing can fill that emptiness but who we are. And who we are, alive in the living present, has no conclusions, no matter how desperately we may feel we need them.

The stream of life continues unbroken, our conclusions notwithstanding, and what seems a tragedy today may tomorrow be shown to have been a blessing. In this regard, Umbrella #7 ("There are no unhappy endings because there are no endings," p. 7) cautions us against a quick faith in the conclusions we feel compelled to reach. Life is always changing, always moving, quietly, beneath the noise of our conclusions, our demands, desires, worries, and fears, flowing inscrutably along in its course, moment into moment, always given and sure in the living present. When we recognize and appreciate this, when we begin to lovingly observe our conclusions about life along with all else rather than identify with them, we find ourselves released into a natural patience in which we do not have to wait for any particular thing to happen in order to feel fully alive.

NATURAL GRATITUDE

As WE PRACTICE LIVING in the present, at times growing forgetful and succumbing to suffering, at times remembering and connecting with the vast sufficiency of our heart, we experience something new: natural gratitude for the simple joy of being. One of the most deeply entrenched delusions we must labor under when we have identified with the endlessly restless willful-mind is that we can find happiness in outer circumstances. This mind readily convinces us that we want to love and be loved, but a careful examination reveals that it is thoroughly dyed in the colors of divisiveness, competition, criticism, ingratitude, and lack. Its slogans are "I'll be happy when ———," "Never enough," and "The grass is always greener." When I was an undergraduate philosophy student at the University of Florida, I made a mistake common among those who, in the throes of infatuation with philosophy, fail to balance the intellect with the heart. Forgetful that the original meaning of the word "philosophy" is "love of wisdom," I naively equated philosophical skill with the ability to tear apart any argument, to reduce any position to a point of contradiction or absurdity. This sort of willful-mind philosophy took me far from simplicity and my sense of natural gratitude for life, the sense that life is somehow inherently good and so much more than enough, and it was many years before I began to remember that it is possible to feel a spontaneous joy for things as they are, a joy that wells up—without arguments or reasons—in the area of the heart.

Since those days, I have come to feel that, while knowledge can be a wonderful thing, intellectual development without a corresponding spiritual maturation can create no end of trouble, hence the expression, "Mind makes a good servant but a bad master." In these terms, the work of recovery is to bring the willful-mind under the jurisdiction of the heart.

In the grief of having been left, gratitude can seem light-years away, of little relevance, a contrived idea. We can hardly imagine being grateful when external conditions are running so contrary to our desires. But often, external conditions merely reflect back to us our own habit of suffering, and it is this inner dimension that is the crucial one. Here we may ask ourselves how happy we were before our partner left. Did we have other reasons for suffering then? This is not an easy question to face. Joyful awareness is not mere resignation, and the mind has a tendency to glorify the past because it has a tendency to glorify whatever it doesn't have so it can feel justified in pursuing it. While we are grieving, we owe it to ourselves to ask when was the last time we felt an active, spontaneous appreciation, simply for the opportunity in the present moment to participate in the miracle of being alive. We *are* alive! How is it that this makes so little difference to us? The mind regards being alive and aware and feeling in the now as not enough because to the mind nothing is ever enough. Its nature is to endlessly play the siren song of its desires, to believe fulfillment is always somewhere else, thereby pulling us out of the simple present into a tumultuous complexity of memories and fantasies, strategies and fears. To the willful-mind, it is not enough that we are alive on a planet that gives us breath after breath, that we are participating in a great adventure of possibilities called "life;" not enough that we have been given personal gifts and talents and strengths and the time to share them so that our own suffering and that of others might be lessened; not enough that we can speak or walk or think, that we are, even in the midst of this suffering, learning to inherit our own open heart, learning to shed a lifetime of posing and isolation so that we may give and receive in even greater fullness.

Gratitude can seem especially foreign when our heart has been broken, if we have been taught that we *should* feel grateful. It is tragic that some of the most beautiful of human sentiments have been reduced to such moralistic force-feeding. This sort of "gratitude" only denies pain. It is far better to begin with an honest acknowledgment of our pain, bitterness, and outrage than to feel such things and, on top of it all, berate ourselves for not feeling grateful! The truth is that a broken heart can hurt so much we may not be sure we want to go on living. Why live when life has become little more than continual pain, regret, and depression? But the desire not to continue living in pain is itself an affirmation of life, a deep recognition that life is more than pain. And in this lie the seeds of a gratitude that has nothing to do with the mind's incessant "should."

Real gratitude arises in our heart when we experience that love's capacity to heal is deeper than the pain of love violated. Of course, when our heartache is at its worst, such a spontaneous outpouring of simple joy in being alive is all but inconceivable. But as we continue to practice compassionate awareness of whatever we are feeling, as we expand into the heart's spaciousness through letting go of control and receiving the present as it is, on its own terms, without the delusions and denials and willfulness of egocentric insistence, this heartache gradually subsides and we begin to feel the wonderful glow of a gratitude that is not gratitude *for* anything, but is original, almost objectless, pervasive. It is the smile that comes of itself when we notice a particularly striking sunset, or see a child standing on his toes to catch a drink at the water fountain. It is a nameless nostalgia that accompanies the first, sudden gusts of autumn, the reassuring voice of a friend we have taken for granted, an unexplainable sense of pride before an approaching storm. This feeling of gratitude is sublime; it is not one we are used to giving much attention to, but it is well worth cultivating, and we can do so by practicing nonjudgment of ourselves and others, compassionate witnessing, inner listening, letting go, and acceptance of the moment, however confusing it may be, however painful.

When we were children, we knew a great deal about simply being, without effort or artifice. You can evoke this grateful, involved awareness by taking a walk through a park or forest, along the beach, anywhere far from daily concerns. When you are there, feel the peace that surrounds the place. As you walk, remember something you once put together or made or planned: a ceramic mug, an automobile engine, a painting, a poem, a special dinner, a vacation trip. Remember how it felt, making something of value. Now, look around you at all you have not made, all you did not have to make. The trees, the ocean, the sky, the earth under your feet, even the workings of your own body— so much has been provided. Take nothing for granted. Breathe each breath into your heart like a gift, giving the gift back with each exhalation. All around you, something great is moving in its course. Understand that you are part of it, you belong to it. Take this understanding to heart.

ON DETAILS

IRONICALLY, we develop a vast heart-awareness by paying full, loving attention to little things, to details. The willful-mind works with generalities and forgone conclusions; it does not like to attend to details because details are the vocabulary of present-ness, and in giving itself to details it surrenders its sense of separateness and opens itself up to the miracle of the moment. The willful-mind does not know how to give itself to the moment. It cannot understand the immediacy of a living present that continuously offers itself to awareness in all its unique, intimate particularity. As we slow the momentum of reactive, willful thinking, however, we begin to notice many little things that went unnoticed earlier. This is how awareness can be gently brought back to its proper balance, its natural center and grounding, from which even suffering may be lovingly noted, taken into the heart, and transformed. We simply step back from the hurried, "on-to-the-next-thing" frame of mind in which we seem to spend so much of our lives and begin to take note of the little things that are immediately present. If this makes no sense to you at this time, it may be because it makes no sense to the willful-mind, with which you have identified. Do it anyway for three days. During that time, watch how incessantly this mind pulls the attention away from the details at hand, into judgments, fantasies, reactions: "This is ridiculous. I must be crazy. What does just watching details have to do with anything?" "That was an interesting detail; I wonder if the next one will be as good." "Uh—I guess I'm not supposed to be thinking about details, just watching them." And so on. This running-all-over-the-place is the mind's business, not ours. Remaining true to heart-awareness, we gently note when we have become caught up in the mind's running commentary and bring our attention gently back to the details of whatever we are examining: the way the sun bathes the vertical blinds in soft light, the sense of constriction in the chest when we remember what it feels like to be left, the smell and sound of fresh coffee percolating. *By turning our attention to the details at hand, we practice fidelity to the living present and open ourselves to that rich, involved awareness that can be found nowhere else.*

It may seem that the details of our immediate experience are far removed from our suffering, and we may feel tempted to dismiss the idea that taking note of them can make any difference. The connection between attention to detail and relief from suffering is certainly not apparent, especially when we are convinced that our suffering can only end when we succeed in bringing outer circumstances into line with our will. It is, however, quite the other way around: Sooner or later, reliance on external conditions condemns us to suffering, while wholehearted participation in the details of our present experience can set us free. An analogy may help here. Let us suppose there is an elixir that can magically cure any ill. Now, imagine a hospital staffed by doctors who do not know about this healing potion. Every day, they treat their patients, many of whom are dying from one disease or another. If you ask each doctor why a given patient is dying, he will give you a brief summary of the patient's condition, and, when the patient finally dies, the cause of death will be written on the death certificate in terms of that particular disease. We could, however, correctly conclude that the "cause" of death in each case is the absence of the healing elixir, simply because if the elixir had been administered death would not have occurred. In the same way, our own failure to awaken to heart-awareness and come to life in the living present takes our life a little each day. Certainly, like the dying patients, we may attribute our suffering to any number of "reasons"—physical pain, being left by our partner, financial woes, and so on. But in every case, reasons notwithstanding, the simple shift in awareness from how we would like the moment to be to how the moment *is,* in all its detail, would carry us beyond suffering to a renewed sense of integrity and wholeness. Sadly, like the doctors in the story, we are unaware of this elixir, of the healing capacity of the heart's openness to the living present, even though it is already in our keeping. If we could take even a taste of it, we would discover with amazement that we do not have to suffer, do not have to be the victims of circumstance as we have believed ourselves to be, that we are walking miracles of wholeness and love. The difficulty comes from the fact that, when we are in great pain, we find it hard to pay full, loving attention. The tendency is to deny, to flee, to push the pain away, and this is natural. But just as natural is the heart's capacity to open, even to our pain, in loving acknowledgment of things as they are. What the willful-mind fights bitterly, the heart can embrace, allowing us to admit our pain into the inherent vastness of loving awareness itself, thereby easing it. At this point, even if we slip back into suffering, it can never be the same, for once we have extended compassion to ourselves, we have begun our recovery, and even our forgetting becomes an occasion for remembering. This can be a wonderful way to approach life, and perhaps, even death, for if we spent our life practicing heartful openness to the moment as it is, death may prove to be but one more miracle waiting to enter receptive awareness. If we can "keep our heart open in hell," as the gifted writer Stephen Levine describes in his book *Who Dies?,* if we can learn to live well despite what may be going on around us, dying itself may become one more opportunity to embrace whatever details present themselves, and wherever death may bear us, we will arrive there with our heart open.

Especially when those who love us see that we have been caught in our suffering for a long time, they are likely to suggest that we "throw ourselves into our work," that we "lose ourselves" in something. The suggestion comes out of the insight that self-consciousness can be painful and a rest from it rejuvenating to some degree, but we must take a close look at which self they are suggesting we lose. As long as we are suffering, we are identified with the willful-mind, and *that* "self" cannot be lost except in finding the heart. The willful-mind is only too willing for us to attempt to deny our pain, to run from it into the distractions of the world, because denial is resistance and it is through resistance that the willful-mind and, along with it, suffering are maintained. We cannot find our way out of suffering by denying the false self, in the same way that we cannot overcome resistance by resisting it or overcome hatred by hating it—this is just second-pain futility. Resistance is overcome by our acceptance of ourselves as we are, including our resistance, and in this profound acceptance, we come home to our heart. Paying attention to the details of the moment has nothing to do with attempting to "lose ourselves" in what is going on around us, which is denial. As long as we seek to lose ourselves, we are still running, though it is not really ourselves we wish to lose, but the pain. By being willing to stop running, by opening our awareness to the details of whatever is going on right now, and letting the moment be exactly as it is, we actually find ourselves. We begin to catch a totally different glimpse of who we are: Rather than the desires with which we have always identified, we see that we are the boundless arena of awareness within which those desires arise, call out for expression, and fall away. Paradoxically, it is by paying attention to the little things that we discover the heart's vastness.

It might be helpful to note here that the willful-mind can simulate this attentiveness to detail, though the whole enterprise is negatively charged. This is why I stipulated that we can develop heart-awareness by paying *full and loving* attention to the details at hand. The willful-mind may pick out this detail or that in order to justify its conclusions, which are invariably judgmental, divisive, or complaining: "She looks nice but her figure isn't right," or "It was a great movie but it was a little too long," and so on. The willful-mind may seize upon the details of a situation to vindicate its complaints, validate its agenda of comparison and lack, evoke resistance, prove a point—in many cases the word "but" appears as the fulcrum of the statements it makes while perpetrating this mischief, and in all cases one can *feel* the intent to be constrictive and negative; often it is obsessive. Full, loving attention to detail, on the other hand, is offered for its own sake, or perhaps it is clearer to say, out of a caring for the present moment, a regard for it as inherently valuable however it may be presenting itself. The heart beholds the details of the living present with a tacit reverence for the fact that anything at all exists; it sees the miraculousness of being in the everyday. Associated with this attentiveness to detail is a feeling of openness and expanding awareness rather than constriction.

One friend and colleague of mine, Charlie Beall, approached philosophy with a wonderful blend of earnestness and humor. Charlie was not a religious man, but the week before his death, he said he had come to realize that God was "in the details." What puzzled him was that he couldn't figure out what a detail was—everything was detail! His heart had opened, weeks before it was to burst physically at a football game he watched, I am sure, in utter delight. He had begun to pay such excellent attention to the life that had always been in him, with him, around him, that even the most ordinary objects had become remarkable. When awareness is inspired by love, nothing is ordinary anymore. It is, as Göethe wrote: "In the end, at last, I have won from you the prize, God's presence in all things." In this sense, the largest self we can become experiences an enormous love for little things. It is this spaciousness and love for details that most characterize the self waiting to escort us out of our suffering.

Here is an exercise that will allow you to focus on the details of the living present and bring your awareness from mind to heart. Have a friend read this to you while you sit calmly and quietly, with your eyes closed, in a comfortable position, or read it to yourself: Take several deep breaths. Slow your breathing, noting how the breath flows naturally in and out of the body. Relax entirely, letting any tension flow out of you with each breath. Continue to breathe deeply, slowly. Now, open your eyes and look around you. The room you are in contains countless details: this book on the shelf, that painting, the play of light and shadows, the feel of the sofa or chair beneath you. Breathe slowly and allow your awareness to settle on a particular detail of the room. Gradually focus on that detail until you feel you are fully conscious of it, appreciating its uniqueness. See it as though for the first time, as something extraordinary and new. Do not be concerned about what this sort of paying attention means. It doesn't mean anything. It is a way of practicing awareness in the present. If your mind pulls you away from direct perception of the detail you have selected, into the stream of thoughts, distractions, and feelings, simply acknowledge the stream and bring your attention gently back to the chosen detail. When you have finished with one detail, close your eyes and, taking slow, deep breaths, relax the body even more. Now, open your eyes and select another detail, quietly taking in its uniqueness. Close your eyes again, breathing even more slowly. You are living in the living present. You are safe in the citadel of now. Open your eyes and slowly, as you are ready, return to your normal pace.

WHEN IN DOUBT, TAKE A DEEP BREATH AND BOW

WHEN MY FRIEND HENRY came back from a week-long retreat in a California Zen monastery, I asked him to sum up what he had learned. He smiled and said simply, "When in doubt, bow." There is a great teaching in this brief statement, and especially if you have worked in vain to bring about a reconciliation with your former partner or to change any situation that has caused you sorrow, you are in a particularly good position to understand it because you will have come face-to-face with a powerfully liberating aspect of reality: the limits of the willful-mind. No matter how much we may have desired something, no matter how vital that something seemed, we were unable to attain it. All our strategic thinking, our heartrending prayers, our most impassioned arguments failed, and we found ourselves facing a hard reality: Our willful-mind is not in charge of outcomes, even when they matter to us tremendously. Willfulness must, in the end, defer to something greater. Omar Khayyam expresses this poignantly in his classic poem, the *Rubáiyát:*

> *The Moving Finger writes; and having writ,*
> *Moves on: nor all your Piety nor Wit*

Shall lure it back to cancel half a Line,
Nor all your Tears, wash out a Word of it. [1]

The impotence of the willful-mind to dictate outcomes, even intensely desired outcomes, is part of what is real in a world where we are privileged to encounter more than merely our own reflection in the waters of experience. Although running smack into this limit can be agonizing, it is also humbling and starts to break down the tyrannical self-centeredness of the willful-mind, which is much like the child who "wants what he wants when he wants it." This breakdown of willfulness can release us from the iron grip of the mind and open the door to our heart. It can teach us the value of bowing, of surrendering to experience and living in a spirit of alert willingness rather than resistance.

Because the life that surrounds and affects us is larger than our will, and because resistance to whatever is present perpetuates suffering, letting go of outcomes is essential to recovery. This letting-go can only be accomplished by practicing a loving, non-judgmental awareness of the mind's activities rather than denying them or identifying with and reacting to them. To be sure, letting-go may not, at first, feel like an act of trust. It can feel a lot more like opting for the lesser of two misfortunes: We may either continue to suffer by insisting on the mind's demands when reality refuses to meet them, or we may let go of those demands, give up, "lose" the uncooperative object of desire. It is a battle between mind and heart, between control and surrender to the miraculous present. At first, we let go simply because we are too exhausted to cling any longer. This letting-go, however tentative, is the beginning of accepting life's larger terms and timing.

Whatever burden we are carrying can be made lighter by our bowing, by our deferring to a gentle awareness of things as they are. If we are feeling lonely, for example, we can bow to our loneliness and extend compassion to ourselves rather than add to

[1]*Rubáiyát of Omar Khayyam,* translated by Edward FitzGerald.

our loneliness with harsh self-judgments. If we feel hatred, we can even bow to our hatred by compassionately regarding ourselves as people who have been hurt enough to hate rather than hating ourselves for hating. This bowing becomes the philosopher's stone of alchemical legend, allowing us to transmute the base metal of mind identification into the gold of heart-awareness. We need only stop resisting to begin to uncover the peace of this awareness in ourselves.

FILLING TIME

AFTER A WHILE, as you grow quieter and more centered in your heart, you will notice that the day is often so emotionally empty that it feels as though you are "doing time." The opening of the heart reveals the willful-mind's imprisonment in the separateness it prizes, and at this point the path of recovery can be steep. Gradually, by regarding the emptiness of your time with compassion, you will find yourself naturally reaching out to fill it. Old interests may return or new ones present themselves. Although you may be aware that motivation is still low, changes in the inner weather will be obvious. This does not mean you will be "over" your former partner or excited at the prospect of meeting someone else right away, but time allowed to be empty begins to seek new fullness on its own, in accordance with the Law of Opposites. The storms will continue for a while, but you will have learned to take shelter in the loving awareness within you, and this will help them pass, regardless of whether or not you are able to feel the truth of this. Again, feelings are not necessarily a good indicator of what is real. They can be very convincing but we need not always identify with what we are feeling. Recovery is deeper than feelings at any given time. Feel what you feel; you are healing all the same.

Clearly, since willfulness is a quality of the mind and all healing occurs in the heart, healing is more than you can will. You
do not will a cut to heal, yet it does so nicely, in its own time.
The heart's healing, too, is largely autonomic and can be helped
best by an attitude of patience and noninterference. Time will
begin to "want" to fill as the inner storm passes. There is no rush;
if you find yourself rushing, take that into your loving awareness
and forgive it, too. The natural replenishment of activity will
almost certainly take months, perhaps years depending on the
depth of the bond with your former partner, how painful the
abandonment was, and how soon you let go of identification with
the willful-mind and open to heart-awareness. Note that letting
time empty is itself a way of beginning to fill time. This is not
a word game. The willingness to do nothing while the storm is
raging, to trust in the healing, fosters acceptance and honesty,
conserves strength, and affirms our identity apart from the
mind's desires. The living present is miraculous, appearing each
moment within the great spaciousness of awareness, and when
we are honest with this, when we stop taking the miracle of here
and now for granted, we experience its incomprehensibility with
a profound sense of "not-knowing" what it is. This, again, is
Shunryu Suzuki-roshi's "beginner's mind," which, in the West,
we see reflected in Jesus's teaching that we must become as little
children to enter the Kingdom of Heaven. Beginner's mind is the
mind that has no idea of what to do, no strategy, no preconcep-
tion, and which therefore is open to the moment. Not-doing does
not mean that things will be left undone, though the willful-mind
may fear this because it cannot understand that the flow of life
is assured even without its authorization. This is something like
the fish thinking that the flow of water through its gills powers
the ocean. The stillness of not-doing, of beginner's mind, makes
it possible for us to hear the voice of the heart, perhaps for the
first time.

Listen to your heart for *specific* guidance. Trust its voice, which
can hardly be expected to give information of any value if we
refuse it beforehand by presuming such information to be inva-

lid. The heart is always one step ahead of the mind as we go through our healing. If you are confused by the fact that there seems to be many inner voices, often conflicting, follow the advice of author and teacher Ram Dass: Be still and listen for the more inner one. Trust that it is the voice of your own, most excellent identity.

BEYOND REASONS:
HOW TO SAY
GOODBYE TO THE PAST

ANYONE WHO ASKED my grandfather the question "Why?" about
anything, took the chance of getting the reply: " 'Y' is a crooked
letter." Joe was a simple, loving man, very present in the here and
now. When he held us on his knee and sang to us, or suddenly
poked us in the ribs, we could feel that presentness, and although
over thirty-five years have passed since he died, he is still very
much alive in our awareness.

Joe's "crooked letter" answer shows he knew what many of us
seem to forget, that reasons often have little to do with the living
present and perhaps should not be quickly trusted. I have noticed
this in the "Why?" I frequently hear when someone asks me to
do something and I decline without automatically furnishing an
explanation. The subsequent request for reasons reveals a great
deal about the asker, for whom the simple, honest disclosure in
the moment, the "no," is not good enough. Raised in the patterns
of insecurity native to the willful-mind, we have been taught to
believe that the truth must be made good enough, must be sub-
stantiated. Sometimes, of course, we may offer reasons as an act
of consideration—to provide added information or express our
caring for the asker by showing that we are not being "unreason-
able" or insensitive. But when we allow explaining to become a

habit, and especially when we give reasons to make our feelings "valid," we have fallen into a kind of dishonesty. When we give reasons because we believe that the moment as it presents itself within us is not sufficient to itself, that it must be justified, we are like the man who shoots arrows randomly into a fence, then goes over and paints bull's-eyes around each of them. Most reasoning is dug up in this way, after the fact. If we pay careful attention to how we typically feel when dealing with this "Why?"—when, for example, we have turned down an offer or an invitation—we may discern that we are stuck in the mind's habit of self-defense, which arises out of its sense of separateness and insecurity. We may notice ourselves saying "I can't" when the truth is "I'd rather not;" "I need" when "I want" is the honest answer. And if we cannot come up with "acceptable" reasons, we may even say "Yes" when we mean "No." What else can we do? We must, at all costs, be "nice," and this "nice" is another word for "victim." By assuming this victim-role, we cut ourselves off from our heart.

Even though this "Why?" makes us uncomfortable, we often submit to it because we still believe that the truth is not good enough, that we need reasons for who we are in this moment. The German philosopher G. Wilhelm Friedrich Hegel wrote "History is written by its victors," and, along the same lines, there is an interesting expression: "Believe what you want; you can always find reasons later." Ultimately, the most honest answer to "Why?" is probably "Because," and all our reasons cover the fact that, when we appear to be explaining why something about us is the way it is, we are really just shooting arrows into the fence.

It is important to distinguish the need for reasons (justifications) from the need to understand our own, deeper motivations because not all "Why?" questions involve flight from the present. There are three significant differences:

1. While justifications miss the living present,
    reaching for deeper understandings of ourselves
    can be a very rich expression of the living present.

2. The need to explain the present is an acquiescence to fear. The willingness to understand our own, deeper motivations is an act of courage—it goes beyond fear.

3. Answering the "Why?" of justification satisfactorily leaves us feeling like we have outwitted an adversary. Answering the "Why?" that seeks self-understanding leaves us feeling liberated, more alive, and more connected.

Telling these two apart can be tricky because the questions we ask ourselves in order to gain a greater understanding of who we are often take the form "Why?" when they are really about the "what" of things: "Why do I repeatedly sabotage my relationships?" for example, is really asking, "What is going on in me right now that makes me want to sabotage my relationships?" This is not a word game. "Why?" tacitly invites us to "figure things out" while "What?" invites us to see what is there. "Why?" sends us spinning back to the past, "What?" calls us to honestly regard the present. Not surprisingly, the willful-mind is much more at home in the "Why?"—in coming up with intricate explanations and theories, most of which serve to keep us from the simple truth of what we are up to, right now, and none of them has anything to do with the heart's ability to simply open our awareness in the here and now and teach us about ourselves. Beneath the camouflage of our cleverness and stories about why we do the things we do are basic, uncomplicated, often touching motivations. It is all there, in the heart, waiting for our acknowledgment—there is nothing to figure out. Deeper self-understanding is really a simple matter of honestly admitting what we already "know" just under the surface of our denial—and this means we must be willing to give up the benefits of denial.

For the brokenhearted, "Why?" can be especially crooked: "Why did she leave?" "Why couldn't things have gone differently?" "Why didn't I try harder?" We can get twisted up in such questions and spend a great deal of time poring over the past and missing the present each moment—the "eye of the needle" that offers the only escape from suffering. In the mind's preoccupation with reasons, with the whys and wherefores created in the dust storms of its endless willfulness, we are far from settling into the simple givenness of things; the awareness within which all our pleasures and problems arise, present themselves, and pass. In this awareness, reasons have no authority because the miracle of the moment is enough. Reasons, in this sense, are nothing more than the endless paperwork of the mind, which forever seeks evidence so that it can try cases. The beginning and end of this effort is just that: effort, resistance, displacement from the spacious present, suffering. In fact, this is one of the hurts we carry: all the times we did not feel good enough just as we were and so came up with reasons. But all this justifying is really a heartless business, and no matter what reasons we come up with, the mind is soon off to find new evidence, new doubts, new interpretations, new strategies, diligently creating more resistance, more fear, more ways to keep us from our heart. Through our misplaced confidence in reasons, we will continue to dredge up the past or, at least, what we call the past. And we will be none the closer to what is real. Reasons have to do with what was, not what is. The living moment has no reasons, or as Blaise Pascal wrote in his *Pensées*, "The heart has its reasons, which reason knows not."

We must let go of our belief in reasons if we are to enter our heart. This includes the belief that life is bad because someone has left us.

Reasons justify our staying stuck. If we are to move beyond suffering, we must let go of them and admit that a great deal of the time we simply do not know why we feel what we feel or why things are the way they are. In this honesty, we come home to ourselves, not as victims of circumstance and frustrated desire, but as receptive, awakened beings. Ironically, we must find our way back to the present—not a half-present that is mechanically, meaninglessly driven by our identification with our desires, but a present that is wondrous and rich and rewarding simply in our very awareness of it, a present in which we are fully present, fully aware. It is an entirely practical matter.

Buddhism gives us a story about a man who lay dying on a road, an arrow in his chest. A scholar came along and saw that the hurt fellow was in quite bad shape; he was soon joined by another person, then another. The three of them stood over the injured man, discussing the situation. The first said, "We'd better not pull it out. He could bleed to death." The second: "It would appear from the angle of entry that the arrow was shot from quite a distance. There are tribes in these parts that use poison. This is a consideration in treating the man." The third took his turn: "It seems to me that the arrow may not have pierced any vital organs. He is still breathing, and there may be enough time to build a stretcher and carry him to town." At that point, a monk happened along. He promptly pulled the arrow out of the man's chest and saved his life. Such is the difference between reasons and reality.

In the same way, while honesty in the present can reveal much to us about ourselves, dwelling on the past or dissecting it in an attempt to figure out why things are the way they are only paves the way for further suffering. Reasons have no power to release us from the constriction of willful-mind identity. We can have the best reasons in the world and still be stuck. Searching the past for answers is a profound denial of the heart, and the heart, while patient, will not be denied forever. It will find ways to let us know when the denial has gone on too long, for the awareness of life as good and expansive in the living present is spiritual air we need to live. Denial gets more and more difficult as we get older, as the armor around the heart grows heavier and our sense that we do not have forever to begin living deepens.

Perhaps the biggest mistake we make when we note how much we are living in the past is trying to force ourselves to stop. Such a tactic uses the language of the heart—let go, live in the present, and so on—but its force comes from the willful-mind, which feeds on resistance of any kind. Again, the heart lights the way with lightness: By extending compassion and kindness to ourselves, we see our being stuck in the past, with all the attendant reasons, recollections, and grievances, as the natural result of a deep hurt. When the willful-mind says "Let go!" it says it with an exclamation mark; it is a military command, not an encouragement. This "psychic punctuation" makes all the difference: It is not the words, but the spirit behind the words that moves us. "Let go . . ." with an ellipsis is whispered, not shouted, and expresses the generosity of the heart within which there is more than enough room for us exactly as we are, even with our longings, regrets, and reasons. As we recover, we come to see that all that matters is the reality of the living moment of kind awareness within which all our reasons, all our being wrong or right, all our thinking and conclusions may at last be blessed and released.

Here is an exercise that will soften some of the rigidity with which you may be holding onto the past. It will allow you to explore in your imagination aspects of your experience you may not be aware of, consider important, or appreciate. It is best to do this exercise in a spirit of lightheartedness. Have a friend read it to you while you sit quietly with eyes closed, or read it to yourself: Let your entire body relax. When you are calm and centered, imagine standing in a great library with thousands of volumes lining the shelves. You notice that these books are not ordinary books: They are all photo albums. It occurs to you that they are photo albums of your own life. Each one is different, each documents a different history. You read the binding of one, which says: "A Teacher to Others." Another reads: "Rich in Friends and Laughter." Another: "Hard Lessons Make a Strong Spirit." You select one, sit down in a large chair, and open the album. As you leaf unhurriedly through it, you see photographs that correspond to actual memories you have, perhaps some that have not come to mind in a long time. Or you see a picture of some new detail of an experience you had assumed you remembered fully, a detail that changes the significance the experience has for you now. Turn the pages without trying to anticipate what you are going to see. Each photograph reflects the theme printed on the binding of the volume. Breathe slowly, taking all the time you want with the volume you have chosen. When you are finished, close the book and take a moment to appreciate that this was an important chapter in your life, a chapter that, in ways you cannot see, will contribute to the chapters yet to come. Put the book carefully back on the shelf, take several slow, deep breaths, just standing there for a moment, then select another volume. Realize that the library is a literal symbol for the wealth of your awareness, which provides you with detailed recollections as you choose and the opportunity to love and affirm them, not for any reason, but because it is your nature. Breathe slowly. Now, open your eyes and notice what is going on inside you, especially in your chest. Feel how the heart is big enough to embrace all of the past in loving acceptance. You do not need to prove anything anymore. What was, was. You are alive in the present.

TRUSTING IN THE LARGER
TIMING OF THINGS

THERE IS a wonderful story about an old farmer in ancient China who worked a small plot of land with his teenage son. They were poor even by the most modest standards. During this time, horses were considered of great value; the richest person in the province owned no more than a dozen of them. One day, a wild horse came galloping into their town, jumped the old farmer's small fence, and began grazing on his land. According to local law, this meant the horse rightfully belonged to him and his family. The boy could hardly contain his joy. His father, noting the situation and the boy's reaction, put his hand gently on his son's shoulder and smiling, said simply, "Who knows what is good or bad?" The following day, the horse, not surprisingly, made its escape back to the mountains, and the boy was devastated. "Who knows what is good or bad?" his father reminded him. On the third day, the horse returned with half a dozen wild horses following. The boy could not believe his eyes. "We're rich!" he cried, to which the father replied, "Who knows what is good or bad?" On the fourth day, the boy climbed on one of the wild horses and was thrown off. He landed hard against the fence, breaking his leg. His father ran to get the doctor and was soon helping him treat the boy, who was crying and lamenting his fate. The old farmer wiped the boy's forehead with a damp cloth, looked deeply into his eyes as though to get his attention in a way he never had, and said, "My son, who knows what is good or bad?" On the fifth day, army recruiters came through the town and took all the young men. Except for one who had a broken leg.

When we are fully, honestly in the living moment, we experience its miraculousness and realize we do not know what the next moment will bring. This means that transformation is possible at any time, and this is the ultimate encouragement. Trust could take hold today, in the next hour, even the next second. We could open to the spaciousness of the heart and let go with our next breath, and while nothing would be different, nothing would be the same, for we would see our life as it has always been as though for the first time. The path of recovery has its steep places, and the beginning of trust is certainly one of them. Trust feels like a "little death" to the willful-mind because it must relinquish control of the present in order to open itself to something greater. Courage is needed, but beyond the constricted "I want what I want when I want it" lies a roomier present filled with a joyful appreciation of life's miraculousness. Uplifted by this appreciation, we no longer feel our disappointments so heavily. We do not give up on life; consequently, we do not experience life as giving up on us. We find we are open to this moment of life, and that this very moment, once we are no longer so identified with our ideas about life, may be more joyful and more fulfilling than we had dreamed precisely because we are open to it, because we have let go of our cherished limitations and adopted an attitude of trust that there is something greater than our idea of how things should be. In order to receive, we must first open our weary fists, and, upon opening them, will we not take just a moment to marvel at the miracle of how hands close and open, how the chapter of our life closes and opens? In this moment of marveling, we have already begun to receive.

Does this mean that, by letting go, we will have specifically what we want, for example, our partner back? Clinging to the hope of this keeps us from letting go, and the heart is not deceived. Letting go means bowing before what is real, being willing to be fully present, to express love even if in new, unseen, perhaps undreamt of terms. When we let go, our will has room in it for a being-willing; it becomes a will to receive as well as to give, to accept, to cooperate. No longer locked within the urgency of our desires, delusions, and self-judgments, we begin to sense the larger rhythms of reality visible only to eyes illuminated by natural patience, courage, and trust: The moment can sustain and fulfill us. Now can be enough. It is not an easy road; but it is most assuredly the one we are on.

MAKING CHOICES

WE MAKE A GREAT FUSS over free will, believing freedom to be the power of deciding which of the willful-mind's desires to satisfy and when to satisfy them, but since we are unaware of our true self, what we call "freedom" is really imprisonment, and what we believe we control in choosing among desires is really controlling us. There is only one true choice, regardless of what is facing us, and it arises in the moment-to-moment awareness of who we are: to stay open or close up, to accept or deny, to allow or resist, to see what is there or impose our willfulness. The choice to close, to deny, to resist, to impose our willfulness is the choice to remain in suffering.

Without awareness of the present, there is no real choice. Like a starving man who roams the streets dying for a meal because he does not know there is a ten-dollar bill in his coat pocket, so do we pursue choices from an awareness of lack and a corresponding unawareness of the abundant present. As long as we are unaware, our behavior is subject to the influences of the willful-mind, intent on maintaining separateness and resistance and, therefore, suffering. We can begin to become aware of some of these subtle emotional and physical patterns that have been dictating our behavior by doing something as simple as paying attention to our breathing. When I first took the time to do this, I detected that on each in-breath, I was experiencing a subtle but undeniable emotional effort. Living had become a chore, and each inhalation expressed constriction and weariness as my lungs tightened with the limit of their capacity for air. On the out-breath, I felt a trace of disappointment, as though each exhalation were a minute sigh. Sometimes, I could discern a slight shudder there. Neither judging nor attempting to do anything about this, I simply paid attention, noting where in my body the effort or disappointment was making itself felt. Gradually, I began to focus on these underlying emotions from the spacious awareness of my heart, with compassion for the pain that had impressed itself even on my breathing. Simply paying attention to these emotional currents began to naturally release them: The in-breath became effortless; the out-breath began to evoke feelings of letting go, expansion, the release of tension. The old way of breathing returned from time to time, but it was not the same. Once I had taken my breathing into heart-awareness, with each conscious breath, I had a choice.

Before we can choose anything, we must become aware that there is a choice. Until we begin to pay attention to the details of the moment, exactly as they are presenting themselves, we will only be able to understand choosing as a willful resolution of conflicting desires. We will not yet have realized that willfulness itself is conflict and that we are quite able, once we reach the heart of the matter, to feel our desires and still choose not to *identify* with them, not lose ourselves in them whether we act on them or not. We can watch them come, make room for them, and watch them go, realizing they are part of the great stream of life presenting itself each moment to our awareness. Until we can choose to respond to desire itself or not, it is our desires that are running the show, not us.

The willful-mind wants one thing and then another; there is no end to it. By identifying with the images it holds before us and anticipating the attainment of them, we feel a powerful surge of excitement and promise. Yet, often after we get what we sought so eagerly, the prize stands forth not as something we "really" wanted, but as something we only "thought" we wanted. The willful-mind recreates the experience in memory, just as it selectively finds reasons when it wants to justify its conclusions, and "This isn't it" ends the matter. Again, we think, the fullness of life is somewhere else. "If only I could get that promotion, I'd be happy." "If only we moved to the islands." "If only I had a more exciting job." "If only my wife understood me." "If only my partner were willing to try again." Lost in a misguided search for a happiness we believe we can bring about by "choosing" outer circumstances, we dig our way deeper and deeper into denial of the present, ignoring the heart, which alone can rescue us from all this running around. We go on to the next chase, the next job, the next partner, the next project, the next city, unaware that "this" will never be "it" as long as we are not situated in the joyful presentness of our true identity.

We only need call to mind the buying habits so many of us have to see the fickleness of what the willful-mind calls "choosing." This quick-change artistry is familiar to professional salespeople, who know that, shortly after deciding to buy something, many people have such strong second thoughts that they are likely to back out of the deal. This "consumer remorse," as it is called, is characterized by a sudden letdown, in part attributable to the loss of buying power, but also to the anticlimax of getting what we believed would fulfill us, only to find its value fleeting. The goods rarely live up to the advertisement, especially when the willful-mind can't wait to move on to the next object of desire. The shopper most susceptible to consumer remorse is the one who buys things as an expression of control, the one for whom the act of purchasing is a fix more than the means to an end. It is amazing how quickly the willful-mind can fly off to questions like "Can I afford this?" and "Do I really need it right now?" and so on, even after an enthusiastic decision to buy. To prevent such second thoughts, a skilled salesperson will congratulate the buyer for his wise decision, summarize the product's benefits, and in other ways offer after-the-sale reinforcement.

Shopping, like eating, smoking, sex, watching television, making money, and many other activities, can become addictive, a form of denial, a distraction that allows us to avoid subtle and sometimes not-so-subtle psychological and emotional realities in sore need of attention. Addictive shopping is usually a chronic pattern of impulsive and unsatisfying spending in which the mind struggles to assert itself in repetitive activity without an awareness of what is really going on. The addicted shopper may purchase a bicycle, for example, fully intending to get out for early morning rides and lose fifteen pounds, but incompatible desires will come up and he will react to them. They will subvert his "choice," and the bike will sit on the porch until the tires go flat, while the only exercise he gets is by going out on other, equally unproductive spending trips. He may feel he "chooses" to go shopping, chooses to buy this or that, and so on, but in reality, because he is unaware of what is driving him, he cannot choose to do otherwise. This shopping "dis-ease" is chronic and progressive, as is all addiction: Bigger and better fixes are needed to keep the willful-mind satisfied and the heart stifled. Fulfillment consists largely of the momentary *respite from desire* and is never reliable because it is built on denial, self-avoidance, delusion, flight from the present, and misplaced effort. Addiction also requires tremendous psychic energy; consequently, it drains the self and leads to exhaustion, which adds to our despair and suffering, especially in those lonely moments when distractions wear thin and reality threatens to come crashing through. So much for what we typically call freedom of the will.

The addicted will is not free, but addictions *can* be broken (as evidenced by members of Alcoholics Anonymous, Al-Anon, Narcotics Anonymous, and other "Twelve-Step" groups). There is even a kind of hidden grace in the chronic and progressive character of addiction because, as the situation worsens, transformation becomes more likely. This may be the meaning of the esoteric saying, "Pleasure is the sickness, sickness the cure," or as Jesus taught, "The affliction is the way." Far from endorsing pain, these statements describe the process made necessary by our own addictive refusal to acknowledge our true identity. Even in the act of taking a fix, however, we know what we are doing. We cannot hide from ourselves entirely; our nature is to be self-aware. In some unacknowledged place, we know of the denial and sense that we are engaged in a self-defeating project because denial actually reinforces the thing it would negate, as in the case of someone who tries to stop smoking by affirming over and over again, "I will not smoke." The mind doesn't hear "not." It can only respond by closing around whatever concept or image is held before it. Consequently, "I will not smoke" only reinforces the idea of smoking.

When we trade our awareness and our ability to make real choices for fixes, we commit the cardinal error of the willful-mind: We settle for entirely too little, taking means to be ends, as in the case of buying for its own sake or winning an argument just to be right. Like Narcissus, we become obsessed with a reflection. Sleepwalking in delusion, we go from reaction to reaction, unaware of the liberation waiting within.

The beauty of heart-awareness is its practicality. When we are clear, when we are out of our suffering and in our heart, our responses can be completely appropriate to the moment. We are "grounded," as one friend puts it. The heart imbues us with a natural command of who we are, an honesty that lends us great presence and credibility. Thus, the basis of the power of real choice is nonseparateness. As long as our choosing does not go beyond the expression of willfulness, we are still on the "outside" of the moment, separate, the unwitting victims of our own unawareness. When choosing becomes a way of remaining within the heart, it is no longer manipulative, no longer merely a reaction to desire. In choosing from the heart, with careful attentiveness to what is present, regardless of what may be rising or falling on the cinema screen of the willful-mind, we embody a tremendous earnestness and a far-reaching influence that touches everyone involved, including ourselves. This unity of heart response is delightfully demonstrated by a true story about Mahatma Gandhi, the great spiritual and political leader of modern India. A woman approached Gandhi one day with her young son, who, it seemed, would not stop eating chocolate. The woman was at a complete loss and prevailed upon the Mahatma for guidance. Gandhi regarded the boy, then said, "Madam, bring him back to me in three days." Three days passed, and the woman again approached Gandhi with the boy at her side. "Excuse me, sir," she said. "You may remember me. Three days ago I brought my son to you, the one who will not stop eating chocolate. You told me to return in three days, which I have done." At this point, Gandhi lifted the boy's chin, looked him squarely in the eye, and said, "Stop eating chocolate." Then he patted the boy on the head and turned to leave. "Sir," the woman interjected, "I don't understand. If this is all you had to say to my son, why couldn't you have said it three days ago?" "Madam," Gandhi explained, "three days ago, *I* was still eating chocolate."

Real choice is not a closing of the willful-mind around something outside of us that it believes will bring us happiness. Real choice includes us; it is an expression of our wholehearted awareness of and participation in the living moment. It opens the way "in" and spontaneously reveals what the moment requires. The willful-mind cannot find this way in. It is by nature an outsider; its language is the language of separateness. Until we allow ourselves to sit in stillness, to gently watch the mind, the emotions, the bodily sensations as they come and go, with forgiveness and acceptance, we will remain in the prison of the freedom we call choosing, a restless spectator of the life in and around us.

TO BED OR NOT TO BED: THE QUESTION OF SEX

I KNEW A MAN who found himself facing a divorce after more than twenty-five years of marriage. He was shattered. His wife had moved out a month earlier, and he called me one day, troubled. When I asked him what specifically was upsetting him, he said that in addition to his grief, he felt he wasn't going to be able to go on much longer without sex. This is a question many of us face when, after years of intimacy with someone, we suddenly find ourselves alone. As we investigate this question of "to bed or not to bed" from the standpoint of recovery, a prior question becomes apparent: Will sex bring us closer to our heart or add to our distance from it? Sometimes, the real motivation for sexual closeness is the desire to ease our emotional isolation, the sense of separateness in which we have been wandering for so long, the feeling of being dispossessed, which our most recent loss has no doubt aggravated. While sex may indeed be the physical expression of a greater, more encompassing emotional bond with another, it can also become a substitute for real closeness, and to the extent that two people pursue it blindly, without an awareness of what is going on in the heart, it can keep them from really touching.

A friend of mine often liked to kid around whenever we went

anywhere together by visibly admiring every beautiful woman who passed by, then turning to me and saying, "She wants me." This happened on a number of occasions, until one day I noticed he never said, "I want *her.*" Sensing there was something to this, I steered the conversation in a different direction and soon asked him how he had felt as a boy. He thought about it and finally answered in a single word: "Unwanted." Because of these old hurts around feeling unwanted, he had as a man, come to equate sexual interest with simply being *wanted*—not necessarily sexually, but wanted in the sense of being accepted, of not being rejected or emotionally abandoned. His heart opened to this insight as he realized how hurt he had been. After this, I never heard him say "She wants me" again. Our humor often covers our pain. So can our sexuality.

Some people who have been left by their partner are repelled by the idea of sex with anyone else. Others want very much to sleep with someone but are emotionally unable or unwilling to wake up with a new partner. Waking up next to someone in the morning is perhaps an even more intimate act than sex; it is an act of perfect trust to have spent the night beside another in the utter privacy and vulnerability of sleep. In this sense, we can see that there is often much more to sex than its physical aspects. Typically, it involves deep issues of trust, sharing, love, bonding—in short, human closeness, that central issue around which so much pain and sorrow seems to have clustered for so many of us.

These injuries have had a far-reaching effect on us. Some of us were abused or neglected as children or grew up with an alcoholic parent; others knew the confusion and grief of living in a home which, for one reason or another, was not emotionally safe. But whatever our personal history, we have all experienced disappointments and losses and, to some degree, withdrawn from the risk of further pain by allowing the armor of denial to build up around our heart. In doing so, we have also cut ourselves off from love, from being fully present in the moment. Until we begin to melt this armor with loving, nonjudgmental awareness,

until we forgive ourselves and others, and enter the healing sanc-
tuary of our heart, sex will remain largely physical and will be
unable to satisfy us deeply.

On the path of recovery, we are like miners digging for gold.
The temptation may be strong for us to run to the first shiny
metal that catches our eye, but we have a deeper purpose. By
digging attentively, we are much more likely to find what we are
looking for, and this approach depends on our willingness to go
slowly, without rushing. Only through the steady self-watchful-
ness that connects us directly with what is real can we bring into
awareness our denied, hurt, and misguided feelings. Once we
experience this, the question of sex takes on a less urgent perspective. Life can easily arrange for another body to be present, but
it is given to us to arrange for our heart to be present.

SPACE AND PLACE

THE FEELING OF HAVING LOST OUR PLACE, of being dislocated in the world, is frighteningly characteristic of modern life. Perhaps this is in part due to the advances in transportation and communication technology that have made us so mobile and desensitized us to distance by giving us electronic substitutes for real closeness. In large numbers each year, we relocate to pursue job opportunities, pulling up roots that take a long time to regrow. This has created a condition of competition between two of the most basic elements of human life: community and livelihood. As a result, we have become a homesick society. We have lost our place.

Place is very different from space: Place suggests fullness, things belonging, order; space is emptiness, nonrelation, chaos. Space is mere possibility; place, the fulfillment of possibility. Wherever we have set up our lives, however we have surrounded ourselves with expressions of who we are, we have created a place for ourselves.

Your partner's leaving may have resulted in your moving out of your place, or perhaps you are still in a home you shared with your partner and are experiencing the disruption of place from that point of view: The bed seems far too large, a hundred silences have replaced the everyday sounds of your partner's moving about, drawers and cabinet doors left casually open are now always conspicuously closed. These details, whether we are aware of them or not, remind us from moment to moment that the intimacy we shared with another is no longer and can lead us to feel homesick in our own house or apartment.

The adage tells us, "Home is where the heart is," and should add, "Seek it there," for while we can have friends over to bring warmth and camaraderie into our house, ultimately we restore our sense of place by coming home to our heart. As we identify increasingly with our heart, we find ourselves undergoing deep changes that affect our sense of belonging or emotional located-ness in time and space, our sense of well-being. Eventually, we can recognize a trace of home even in our alienation, since there is nothing the heart cannot make a place for. Initially, this transi-tion can feel like "losing it;" it is, after all, the loss of identifica-tion with the willful-mind, which is no longer boss and certainly doesn't like being out of work. This is why we spend so much time avoiding it, hiding in the world of our desires. Nevertheless, facing both the joy and the fear of our own vastness is the only way out of the hell of our suffering. The willingness to make the transition from addictive identification with the willful-mind and dependency on external circumstances requires great cour-age, involving as it does nothing less than the destruction of patterns that have been practiced, in many cases, for decades and are the only reality we *know.* Beyond these patterns, however, waits a sky unimaginably clear and wonderful, and not sky as space, but sky as the inscrutable openness of awareness itself, the edgeless backdrop within which our world manifests itself and is given to us in each moment.

Here is an exercise that will allow you to tangibly experience the difference between space and place. Remember what your home looked like just before you moved into it. It was empty, raw space, the mere possibility of place. Now, looking around you, notice how you created a sense of order within which to live. The living room, your work area, the arrangement of paintings and other decorations—all these express some aspect of your own sense of place and belonging. If you like, choose one aspect of this order to rearrange: Reduce its present organization to raw space again; for example, remove all the paintings from the wall or clear the desk. Notice how the space "asks" to be imbued with place, how unfinished space is by contrast. Slowly, thoughtfully, reorganize the area you have selected so that it contains *more* place than before. When you are finished, step back and look at what you have done. Note that it pleases you. Place is naturally rewarding and, despite circumstances, you are empowered to create it again and again.

PRAYERS THAT DON'T WORK, PRAYERS THAT WORK

You won't find an atheist in a foxhole, the saying goes, and I don't doubt it. Times of crisis always seem to fire us up with that spirituality that sees God as employable and open to striking bargains. "God, just bring my partner back and I promise I'll———." Though it is understandable that we cry out for help in this way when we are in despair, and though such crying out may have therapeutic value, praying in this way does not seem to work much of the time. Imagine the prayers of those who lived during the Inquisition, during Stalin's murderous "purge," during the Holocaust; of people who this very day are starving and watching their children starve. This is not to diminish the genuine tragedy of those who, having been left, call out to God for some kind of remedy, but rather to point out that, most of the time, God does not seem to be taking such calls. And if indeed God did answer our most pained requests, would we be at any less of a loss to understand why the prayers of so many others in situations of enormous need and suffering, possibly far greater than our own, receive no response? What sense would such an arbitrarily cooperative God make?

Here, an old theological question presents itself: How could God allow me to suffer so much? How can day after week, week after month go on with no answer to desperate prayers for a reconciliation, for one more chance to rebuild a life with this person I love so? This question appears in classical literature in this form: "How can we reconcile the evil in the world with a God who is supposed to be both all-loving and all-powerful?" Clearly, there is evil (seemingly unjustified suffering) in the world. If God is all-loving, He must not be powerful enough to stop it. If, on the other hand, He is all-powerful, he must not care enough to stop it. It is a Gordian knot for the believer who holds to the traditional Judeo-Christian God.

Some suggest that God's power has been compromised by His having given man free will, an act that necessarily limited Him. Because people are free to choose good or evil, they sometimes choose evil. God cannot stop it without denying human moral integrity. Others suggest that there isn't really evil in the world, only seeming evil, perhaps in the same way that the monster who chases us in a dream turns out to have been only a seeming monster when we wake up. Even death, the argument concludes, is actually a waking from the dream of life, in which suffering seems real but ultimately is not. Another explanation says that there is a hidden purpose behind our suffering, a purpose that will be revealed to us at a later time, perhaps in an afterlife.

These are interesting answers, but none of them is of much help to anyone caught in the suffering of a broken heart, for the fact that someone we trust is free to choose to injure us is in no way edifying or comforting. Neither does it do any good to "metaphysicalize" away the hurt by saying it only seems to be real, for it indeed *seems to be*, and, in our immediate experience, it is as real as real can be. The fact that it may be seen later in a different light cannot discount its experienced reality now. Finally, there is little consolation in the idea that some hidden purpose may be revealed to us later, for what purpose would mitigate such a loss?

Having been abandoned, having done everything within our power to influence the situation, and still finding ourselves stuck in chronic, often overwhelming pain, we naturally call out to

God for help. In this way, a deep "cosmic" rejection is set up that may infiltrate our whole belief and value system, wreaking havoc. Indeed, it can seem that God is "on the side" of our flown partner, for despite frantic cries for support, presence, an answer, we find only an awful unresponsiveness from both.

Even if our prayers are eventually answered in the way we want, or in some surprisingly better way, the answers are often delayed beyond our ability to postpone inner changes, changes that make us different people praying for new things. In any event, there are strong forces at work in both individuals caught up in an abandonment experience—the one who leaves and the one who is left. It cannot be very easy, even for a god, simply to snap his fingers and change the movie to a happier one upon request. Regarding the sort of prayers that don't work, no one I know of has written a more concise, sensitive, and honest apologetic than Rabbi Harold Kushner in his book *When Bad Things Happen to Good People*. Prayers that ignore the complexity of the emotional realities involved do not seem to work. Prayers that solicit help by offering to give something up—"bargain prayers"—do not seem to work; God is apparently not particularly susceptible to human bribes, no matter how sincerely offered. Prayers that ask God to suspend the natural order of things, including their inherent timing, do not seem to work. Selfish prayers, offered without regard for the possible effect on others, do not seem to work. We appear to be stuck then, with an absent partner, a silent God, and a great number of prayers that don't work.

Are there prayers that do work? There are, and again, Rabbi Kushner's book is highly recommended. One can pray successfully for the strength to get through the crisis. One can pray successfully for understanding that will lessen the pain. One can pray successfully to forgive another rather than dwell on harms done, since forgiving is healing to the forgiver and dwelling on harms done only does further harm. One can pray successfully for courage, guidance, faith, renewed self-confidence and self-appreciation. One can pray for support and the wisdom to recognize and receive it. And one can certainly be grateful for the answers to such prayers, which are often striking in the difference they make. Gratitude itself is a form of prayer, a great receptivity that attracts blessings. One can even be grateful for being able to feel gratitude, since gratitude is a profound expression of heartfelt presentness and as such a powerful healing force.

What is most revealing here is that the prayers that seem to work all involve *self*-transformation, while those that fail are invariably directed at changing *circumstances*. Perhaps there is an instruction in this. Spiritually, our business is, first and last, the condition of our own heart. When we keep our attention there, we find there is help, there is guidance, there is a response, and the results can be astonishing. But, when we keep our attention on the world of events and circumstances, we often find we get the same answer anyone might get if he insisted on asking the wrong questions. This is why, when we pray, we do well to pray humbly. "Thy will be done" is said to be the highest form of prayer, and it is, of course, a statement of open willingness to cooperate and follow, rather than a request or a demand. What the willful-mind would coerce God to do, the heart is already receiving. When we are looking for something we have lost, it is best to search where there is light.

LOOKING AHEAD

WHEN A BOND OF LOVE IS BROKEN, and especially if we come to believe there is little or no chance of reconciliation, we may feel a strong urge to find someone new. This deserves careful examination. There may be a considerable amount of unfinished business with your former partner, whether or not a gradual, loving resolution is possible at this time. We can, however, work through unfinished business with those we love even if they are not around, even, in fact, if they have died. Losing someone we love in any form can leave us with a great deal to grieve about and forgive. Taking time to do so not only brings us more into our heart; it also makes it possible for us to enter into a new bond with greater awareness. A precipitous involvement, on the other hand, can interfere with the expansion of awareness into the heart, making it less likely that we will be able to maintain the focus needed to feel our feelings and be finished with them, to really let go. Recovery is difficult enough without the demands and distractions of a new partnership for which we may not be ready. Our first responsibility is to ourselves, to find our wholeness.

Generally, it is probably wiser to go slowly than to jump into a new relationship because precipitous action can serve to keep our own self-defeating patterns hidden from us. To illustrate with a true story: A woman called the local Alcoholics Anonymous chapter in tears because she couldn't find her husband and was afraid that he had gone on another binge. After listening to her story for ten minutes, the phone counselor asked her if she had been married before. "This is the third time," she said. "They were all alcoholics, weren't they?" the counselor asked. "Why, yes," she said taken aback. It is not surprising that this experienced counselor knew, by the way she told her story, that it was an old one. Patterns of self-defeat, even self-destruction, are nothing new, and they occur in the lives of many millions of people who will never get drunk or take drugs. Chronic and progressive, they replay throughout life while the scenery of names, places, and faces changes, dictating sad outcomes and setting the stage for more of the same in each new effort. Certainly, it is possible to transcend these addictive patterns just as it is possible to overcome addiction to drugs, but a deep sincerity is needed, and as Scripture reminds us, the "harvest is rich but the workers are few." Because self-transformation requires us to courageously open our heart to the miraculous, uncontrollable present, and because we are so identified with the willful-mind that we are terrified of our heart, we settle for quick fixes and do not reach for a healthier way of being until our suffering becomes almost unbearable. At such times, we are eager to open ourselves to healing. But recovery is more than a treatment for crisis. It is a way of life.

Especially if you are aware of recurrent, destructive patterns in your history of past loves, you may want to put off getting involved right away and seek out one of the many support groups available for those who wish to recover from addictive living. Again, a good friend or therapist who is a skilled listener and whom you trust deeply can provide invaluable support and perspective. Until we begin the vital work of recognizing and letting go of our addictions through embracing and forgiving them each moment, there can be no real looking ahead because the future will be nothing more than a replay of the past.

ON YOUR SPECIAL CIRCUMSTANCES

CLEARLY, PEOPLE SPLIT UP for innumerable reasons, leaving behind them a diversity of situations, and you may be wondering how to apply the ideas in this book to your own, unique circumstances. Perhaps your husband or wife has left you after many years of marriage. You may have been left suddenly by a partner you had no idea was even thinking of leaving, or by someone with whom you've been locked in argument and struggle for years. Your partner may have left you in order to be with someone else. Perhaps there are children or stepchildren involved in your situation.

Regardless of special circumstances, the process of recovery is essentially the same. In order to move beyond shock, grief, or anger, we must engage whatever inner and outer resources we can and use them to practice offering compassion and forgiveness to ourselves and, as we become ready, to others. In practical terms, *while situational differences have to be accommodated,* they are irrelevant to the real work of recovery in the same way that how a person breaks his leg is largely irrelevant to what he must do to take care of it. Each of us must learn to recognize when action is to be taken, to refrain when there is nothing more we can do, to let go of the payoffs inherent in the habit of suffering, and, most importantly, to begin to wake up to whatever part we are playing in our suffering and practice making more enlightened choices.

It is not easy to recover. But then it is not easy to continue suffering, nor is it particularly easy to be alive at all, to deal with the demands and complexities each of us must face every day. This is why it is so important to remember that recovery is possible. It is not even far away; we have much greater resources than we use and are so often our own worst enemies, keeping ourselves all but paralyzed with fear, worry, doubt, and indecision. It is good for us to ponder the idea that recovery is possible for us, that we can start to feel better than we may feel today, that things change and that we can, if we allow ourselves to, change with them and change for the better. By becoming willing to do so, to put into practice the ideas offered in this book no matter how we may be feeling on a given day, we avoid the risk that the mind will seize upon our special circumstances as an excuse for keeping us stuck.

Wherever we find ourselves at this moment, however depressed or angry or hopeless we may be feeling, we can begin. We can loosen the fist of the willful-mind in the gentleness of witnessing. We can at least try to have a little kindness for ourselves rather than stay locked in protest and grief. Here and now is given, always given. Here and now is the perfect point of departure for our healing journey. Let whatever special circumstances you may be in mold themselves to the vital inner work of opening heart-awareness. Give it a little time and you will see your patience and willingness working gradual wonders.

THE RECOVERY CHECKLIST

THERE IS A GREAT DEAL you can do to take care of yourself while you ride out the daily storms. Here is a checklist of ideas:

1. I take some time to remember that the worst of my feelings are still just feelings. They do not accurately portray reality or delimit what is possible for me.

2. I am patient with myself and my troubled emotions. I remind myself that all situations and circumstances change. I take as much time as I need.

3. I accept my negative thoughts and feelings as part of the healing process, not as reality-indicators. I do not get negative about being negative.

4. I welcome the support and loving attention of my friends and family.

5. I do considerate, entertaining, and exciting things with a friend or by myself.

6. I choose to live creatively, not reactively.

7. Anything is possible for me. I have a right to believe this and act out of this belief.

8. I do not have to make emotional decisions right now.

9. I deserve to be appreciated. I will accept appreciation without embarrassment or excuses.

10. I affirm my beauty and worth daily.

11. I promise to take myself to a new restaurant for dinner, read a book I've been wanting to read for a long time, or take that class I've been interested in but never got around to.

12. I make a pact with myself to extend patience, compassion, and understanding in my own behalf, just as I would for a hurt friend.

13. I use my creativity to do something, no matter how small, each day to affirm the goodness of my life, *regardless of how I may feel.*

Using this checklist will help you reclaim at least some moments of joy each day, and these will increase as the recovery process continues. Remember to be gentle with yourself. Take plenty of time. Trust the healing forces within you.

LIVING
WHOLEHEARTEDLY

All goes onward and outward, nothing collapses,
And to die is different from what any one sup-
posed, and luckier.

—WALT WHITMAN
Song of Myself

On a clear day, rise and look around you,
and you'll see who you are.
On a clear day, how it will astound you,
that the glow of your being, outshines every star.

—JAY LERNER
On a Clear Day
You Can See Forever

THE CLEAR SKY OF SELF

LOVING AWARENESS in the living present is like a clear sky within which everything moves in its course, ourselves included. At the same time, within this spaciousness is a wonderful earthiness and balance: When we are in our heart, we are grounded, connected with the details of bodily experience, its physical and emotional ebb and flow—this pain, that pleasure, the warmth, the texture, the touch, all of this, each moment, exactly as it is. In this sense, sky and ground, heaven and earth, join forces within us and we become spaciously aware of our body somewhat less personally than before, as one more cloud moving through the great vastness of the heart. From this higher angle of vision, this openness, we realize that, even when we are filled with grief, recovery is proceeding. We are freed from the willful-mind's insistence that the moment be other than it is. When the self defers to what is real rather than insisting on wearing the straitjacket of the mind, it experiences its own openness as physical release, roominess, and joy.

From time to time, the mind will pull us away from the heart. One of its great deceptions is the idea that the heartfelt joy of open awareness itself is something *desirable!* This of course, turns the living present into one more thing to acquire, to strive for, which makes it seem distant and sets it apart from the self once more. With a little practice, we may embrace this desire for the present in the very moment of desiring, thus again becoming aware of ourselves in the living, loving moment of complete acceptance, honesty, and forgiveness.

When I was teaching philosophy at a community college, I came upon a remarkable fragment of verse in a collection of interesting quotes and comments—a definition of the word "forgiveness."

> *Forgiveness:*
> *The fragrance the violet leaves*
> *on the heel that crushes it.*

I remember feeling nothing but an odd disconnection, as I read and reread these lines. Looking at the bottom of the page, I noted that the verse had been anonymously written by the inmate of a mental institution, and I thought: I can read such words and feel nothing. How much beauty and richness do I miss each day because I am not in my heart to receive it? And I considered that this absence, too, is a kind of madness.

Somewhere along the line my enthusiasm had been extinguished. I had been suffocating in years of willful-mind constriction and didn't even know it. Some of my students showed this same numbness to life, a kind of pervasive and chronic lack of passion or exuberance. The feeling I got talking with them was that they had been punished when they were little by being sent to their rooms and that part of them had never come back out. I understood this about them because I sensed the same constriction in myself, a quality of being locked in, as though a great deal had been pressed into a small space. Somehow, we had been put out of touch with the spirit of exploration, discovery, and participation so visible in babies and toddlers. We were not really present, not grounded, not "well in our skin." Like a tree cut at the roots, we had withered and could not reach up, could not branch out, could not grow into the clear sky of self.

We hold onto our suffering through a willful refusal to identify with our heart's inherent enthusiasm, joy, responsiveness, and compassion. When someone has hurt us and our suffering seems so justified, it is hard for us to realize we are shut down, hard for us to catch ourselves in the act of self-obsession because we have accepted a constricted reality in order not to feel. A numbed, wandering existence of reaction to desire seems preferable to swimming up through so much pain to the surface where we may live again. In moments of great suffering, however, when pain itself has pushed us beyond numbness, we are closer than we may know to our healing. These are the moments when we are humbled, when we realize that what is given in the living present is so much greater than the mind's self-pity, no matter how justified it may seem. When we directly experience life again in this way, even if only for a moment, we glimpse that the whole of being is secure in its course, quite independent of our little will. For the mind, this moment is, at last, the acknowledgment that it is not the ultimate authority: It finally grasps the obvious, that all around it is something greater than itself. Experienced this way, as proceeding miraculously in its own right, life holds up a mirror that reflects the vulnerability, foolishness, struggle, the predicament, the bittersweetness, the tragedy and comedy of being human, and we may feel we have seen ourselves for the first time. When we become aware of the self that dwells in our heart, beneath the turmoil of suffering, we find we are face-to-face with love, and we experience the goodness of life directly.

One of the visible changes that takes place in us as we continue to open to our heart is an increasing compassion and empathy for others. We recognize them as part of the one miracle, moving in their course, apart from whatever "use" the willful-mind may or may not have for them. In this receptive state, we experience a spontaneous love for others that flows from our love for being, pure and simple. This love far surpasses the mind-driven race for gratifications we had called "love" earlier. It is not difficult to love in this way when we behold the face of the miracle we call life—indeed, it is impossible not to. What is difficult is to recognize the miracle for what it is, to step out of the melodramas of the mind and see what the moment has placed before us.

If we continue to live within the demands of the willful-mind, in pursuit of some idea of happiness or at least relief from the anxious suspicion that our life has become empty and meaning-less, we are gradually imprisoned in our armor and cannot break through to the only thing that can redeem us: life, not some idea of life, but life itself—miraculous, engaging, ever sufficient. Many of us can physically feel this armor, the weight around the heart that holds us down and keeps us from taking flight into our own, spacious identity. Sometimes we become aware of it when a relative dies, and, to our dismay, we feel little or no grief, as though someone had turned us off like a switch. Even our own children may bring us little joy if long-standing identification with the divisive mind has put us out of our heart. We may look at them and wish we could feel our love for them. Inside, we are in exile. We are not grounded, not in our body. We do not feel the feelings we know are in us, somewhere, lost. Many years after the fact, we may suddenly find ourselves weeping for the lost relative or feeling a wave of regret for all the times we could not feel the beauty of our children or our parents and so did not tell them and thank them and celebrate them. Something in us knows that we do not have forever to open up, to find the sky and live.

It is important to begin. Without forcing change, we must stop at some point and enter the moment, loving ourselves regardless of what we can and can't feel, watching the mind with merciful detachment, noting the details without identifying with them. In these ways, we begin to strengthen the muscles of awareness and ground ourselves in the living present. Gradually, a wonderful healing takes place that has nothing to do with circumstances or conditions.

Forgiveness:
The fragrance the violet leaves
on the heel that crushes it.

When I think back to those days of teaching college, I am grateful for having awakened, at least somewhat more, to the miracle of my own heart. Now, I understand why I found the forgiveness verse so moving. We are all the violet, crushed by the sorrow and bitter disappointments we carry. And it is this very crushing that releases our heartful awareness, our human essence, the fragrance that opens up around us, subtle and rich, that generously and naturally overflows with the fullness of itself.

WILLINGNESS

As the practice of recovery becomes established in our lives, our joy increases, and we find our mind falling into our heart. Then we are, as my friend Kären says, "thinking with the heart." Compassion becomes not merely a nice quality we should have, but an ever-present condition of awareness: Compassion for ourselves, compassion for others—it is all the same; there is no longer any *essential* separateness. We see someone in pain and our heart goes out to him because we have known pain. Or we see someone stuck in suffering and know that, whatever the details of the drama, he is suffering because he has not come home to his heart. A gentle letting-go into the ever-sufficient present would end or ameliorate his suffering, but he cannot find the present because he does not know he has lost it through unawareness. So our heart goes out to him, too, because we have made room in our heart for ourselves, for all we have come upon in ourselves, including the many times we forgot to come home to our heart. In the clarity of this acceptance, of each moment we remember, we come home again and again.

The heart is most unlike the mind in the expression of *will*, for the mind is *willful*, while the heart is *willing*. Willfulness sees the world in terms of logical order, control, aggressiveness, literalness, the visible, direction, striving, tenacity, and initiative. Willingness encompasses intuition, trusting, letting-go, openness, nurturing, symbolism and association, the hidden, yielding, and feeling. It is interesting to note that, although these terms are not necessarily gender-linked, they have become so through conditioning: Women have been taught to express their willingness more than their willfulness; with men, it is the other way around. Nevertheless, given the predominance of mind identity and our society's emphasis on acquisition as the key to personal happiness, especially since the sixties, there has been an increasing tendency for both men and women to accentuate willfulness at the expense of willingness.[1]

Willingness is natural to the heart, and it is grievous that we have lost sight of this in the oblivious pursuit of our delusions. Though many in our society seem to be awakening to the great importance of willingness, for the most part we are still obsessed with planning, persuading, designing, doing, achieving, controlling, and taking, and we are out of touch with waiting, watching, listening, acknowledging, accepting, trusting, letting-go, and receiving. Nothing points this out as dramatically as when our denial—the consummate manifestation of willfulness—begins to fail us, and the mind starts fighting for its life. We may finally be

[1]In general terms, suffering arises out of a lack of willingness. As a rule, our society conditions women to deny their natural willful potential, men to deny their natural capacity for willingness, but what is especially worth noting here is that both involve denial. Consequently, both foster resistance and further the mind's domination of the heart. Both passivity and aggressiveness are manipulative and, in the sense that the terms are used in this work, constitute a lack of willingness, that is, the willingness to enter the living present without attempting to deny its fundamental newness and uncontrollability. Any woman whose self-denial prevents her from asserting her individuality, standing up for what she feels and believes, and so on (the willful principle) is lacking a healthy relation to heartfulness in the same way that a man who denies his capacity for willingness is not in healthy relation to his own heart. The balanced, grounded psyche depends on an honest acknowledgment of things as they are, and therefore an absence of denial in any form. Both passivity and aggression deny the fundamental spaciousness and honesty of heart-awareness. Clearly, when we talk about the willingness that leads beyond suffering, then, we are not talking about a passivity that, in being self-deprecating and manipulative, is essentially a covert form of willfulness.

forced to admit that we cannot make our life work, that we need help, at which point we have begun to see things as they are. This admission of powerlessness is the first step of willingness.

It is typically very hard for us to let go of our willfulness because doing so means accepting the reality we feel pressed to deny, and this runs contrary to the very underpinnings of the mind. When we suffer from abandonment, for example, we are often unwilling to accept the fact that there is absolutely nothing we can do to bring about a reconciliation, sometimes despite many months, even years of tremendous effort. Any person so devoted to futility would do well to examine his heart for what his motivation might be and take an honest look at why he has such an investment in ongoing pain. Such "loyalty" demonstrates the perseverence of the mind, which is the real "prodigal son," the willful member of our inner household who is in flight from the wisdom of love. In the end, suffering will bring this mind to the point where it can yield, perhaps must yield, learn its lessons, and turn toward home.

When we pay loving attention to whatever is going on in and around us, we enter a state of willingness and find ourselves letting go, trusting in the larger timing of things, honoring the Law of Opposites, listening for inner guidance, praying for the wisdom and strength not to resist life. When we let go of our resistance to life, we find life's resistance to us diminishing. This opening up to the living present, exactly as it is, allows us to inherit our own fullest identity.

We have suffered enough. It is time we woke up to our wholeness. Although the willful-mind cringes at the thought, sometimes it is best to give up on our plans, ideals, and desires; sometimes giving up is long overdue. When we have done everything we can think of to help bring about a reconciliation and have failed, what good does it do to keep doing? As long as we are possessed by willfulness, we cannot enter the heart's openness and heal. Desire for release from suffering, of course, only compounds the mess nicely, adding a kind of "third pain." Remember, we transcend suffering by opening our heart to it, by noting it compassionately, by admitting it, entering it, and accepting it—not by struggling against it. Our pain and suffering are part of the living present that needs our willingness, not our denial or judgment. If we are to be uplifted, we must first become light.

Willingness may come in a moment of exhausted surrender, as a calm letting-go, or simply as a new interest in following rather than leading. When we stop willing and *become* willing, things begin to change, sometimes with striking speed. Addiction relaxes its fists; the phantoms of the mind, having no real life of their own and no longer sustained by our identifying with them, evaporate as we recognize that we do not know as much as we thought we did, and that the miracle of who we are is something better trusted than controlled. For a while, this may be the only honest conclusion: We do not know. Perhaps for the first time, we may accept how little we have ever known, and this acceptance alone can release a great deal of our stored pain, for we have tried so hard to know, to be right, to be good enough, to be safe. We open ourselves to our innocence, to our not-knowing, and begin to embody a natural humility, which, more than anything else, marks our entry into the heart. We allow our cup to be emptied. We become as children again. We are ready to receive.

The shift to heart-awareness can provide us with a higher angle of vision than we have when we are stuck in our pain. This is illustrated by a true story about Victor Frankl, the gifted psychiatrist who founded logotherapy. Frankl found he was unable to help an elderly physician who had come to him severely depressed. The man had lost his wife two years earlier and was inconsolable. After listening to the widower, Frankl asked him what it would have been like for his wife if he had died first. The man replied, "Oh, for her this would have been terrible; how she would have suffered!" Frankl replied: "You see, Doctor, such a suffering has been spared her, and it is you who have spared her this suffering; but now you have to pay for it by surviving and mourning her."[2] The man left Frank's office at peace, healed by a greater awareness that made his pain a gift to the woman he loved. Frankl had helped him open himself up to his heart in a way that made his pain an expression of the very love he had lost. This demonstrates how healing can spontaneously occur when awareness expands into greater awareness and adopts a heartful perspective.

Here is an exercise in willingness: Make a list of interests and abilities you have not cultivated. Put down whatever comes to mind, no matter how incidental or unimportant it may seem. You will probably find yourself thinking of activities that never occurred to you before. Let the list build slowly over a few days as ideas come to you. There is no need to hurry. When you are in a quiet and receptive frame of mind, sit down with the list and take several slow, deep breaths. Close your eyes and enter the silent spaciousness of your heart for a few minutes. Now, open your eyes and look over the list. The ideas before you represent the hidden side of your nature, your capacities rather than your accomplishments, things you may be willing to do rather than things you willed to do. Each idea is an invitation to make some untapped aspect of yourself real, exactly as you once did with all your present accomplishments. Let the list speak to your heart. One or two of the ideas will probably appeal more than the others. If this doesn't happen, develop the list for another couple of days, then consider it again. Eventually, something will stand out. Your own willingness has revealed this to you. Trust it. Over the next day or two, think about how you might bring this activity into your life. Follow through and see what happens.

[2]Victor Frankl, *Man's Search For Meaning* (New York: Washington Square Press, 1970).

CAN WE STILL LOVE OUR FORMER PARTNER?

EVEN THOUGH YOU HAVE BEEN HURT BADLY by your partner, you may still genuinely love him or her and want to continue your commitment despite the lack of reciprocity. This means you may want to go on believing in the possibility of an eventual resolution and reconciliation. Well-intentioned friends are likely to tell you this is a sign of a lack of self-respect and, depending on your relationship, it may be; but it may also be a sign of a love that is so deeply creative and powerful that it refuses to react to circumstances. Such a position is a double-edged sword: On one hand, it may sound the depth of your love and, to a large degree, how much you have been able to avoid reacting. On the other hand, a commitment to unrequited love is a formula for ongoing pain, and past a certain point the willingness to remain in such pain raises serious practical questions about whether one is in fact *able* to let go. This is an intensely private matter, and anything short of complete self-honesty, in this regard, is a ticket to hell. If you are clinging to your partner addictively, you will suffer no matter how much you romanticize your loyalty. By choosing to continue loving your absent partner as a partner, you risk a perilous liability that should be understood well: Such an unequal situation leaves you teetering in the precarious balance of waiting while at the same time, somehow, living your life. As long as you choose to remain open to an eventual reconciliation, you must find a way to keep a candle alight in the window without burning down the whole house. That is, you must come home to the living present and live.

> *If waiting keeps you from living life fully, you are caught in an addiction.*

It is extremely difficult, in practical terms, to maintain such a balance, and probably becomes more difficult with the passing of time. The choice between waiting and going on is fraught with emotional peril. You may ultimately have to recognize that the love you have lost indeed can never be replaced, but that this means, not that you ought to hold out for reconciliation, but that love is a wondrous event that goes on despite the absence of mutuality, perhaps despite even the injury inflicted by abandonment. In fact, the inability to be at peace with a love because that love brings no tangible returns is, though infinitely understandable, a hangover of the willful-mind. If you have done everything within your power to work out a reconciliation and your partner still does not want to join you in a rebuilding your bond, the greater act of love is to let go: If you love her, you will hear her and release her to go on to her own happiness, however she envisions it. And if you love yourself, you will open your own life to more than suffering. The image of the candle burning in the window is so romantic, so touching, that we can want to hold on to it far longer than is wise. Up to a point, it is difficult to say which is harder, holding on or letting go, but when the mind reaches saturation and the heart begins to open, we find ourselves at the threshold of a love that is no longer waiting for anything.

In principle, deciding to remain open to an eventual reconciliation does not preclude going on with your own life, though again the matter is slippery. If and when the timing is right, your former partner can just as easily contact you whether you're glad to be alive or still grieving. And if, in healing and opening up to life again in terms other than those of the earlier partnership, you should meet someone else or discover previously hidden possibilities for joyful living without a partner, you may be surprised to find that your love for your former partner has evolved beyond possessiveness and conditions and that you feel closer than ever despite physical or circumstantial distances.

"I love you so much I can't live without you," taken as a description of reality, is a serious delusion. Genuine love, unlike the so-called love of the willful-mind, is soft—the open hand, not the frantic fist. As hard as it may be to put into practice, love is ever concerned with giving itself to the moment, not getting back. Having been left, we will naturally be sad, heartbroken for a while. But we should not, for our own sake, indulge in the damaging confusion that love will prevent us from living. The simple fact that we feel pain does not have to make us martyrs; there are better roles for us to play. We must pay attention and let the feelings come and go as feelings do if they are witnessed and left alone.

ONLY ONE HEART IN
THE WHOLE WORLD

IT IS CLEAR that the heart does not wear a watch. Some experiences, although over in a few moments, can stay with us a lifetime. One night I was walking along a fairly deserted campus. It was late, an autumn chill was blowing across the plaza that, earlier that day, had been filled with students reading, sleeping, tossing frisbees. I felt particularly lighthearted; the night seemed perfect and I felt a perfect part of it. Then I noticed someone approaching from off to my right. Walking into the penumbra of a streetlamp, this person was revealed to be a young, Asian man. "Hello," I said, smiling. He hesitated. "Do I know you?" he asked. "No," I said. Then, feeling the unfortunate need to explain friendliness to strangers, those people our parents told us never to talk to, I added, "I was just being friendly." "Oh," he said, smiling back, "then I know you."

In the long run, the willful-mind's obsession with being separate is futile because the true self is the heart and there is only one heart in the whole world. Eventually, as we accept that we cannot control love, we see the world not as a huge restaurant put here to serve us, but as a miraculous and joyful presence that fills each moment with the wonder of itself, a wonder to which we belong. In this awakening of our own heart, we receive life in abundance; we overflow, giving of ourselves in the form of the very love we were so desperate for the world to give us. We understand, finally, that as long as we seek primarily to get, as long as we remain locked in the mind's reactive way of being, we set into motion a series of events that is doomed to end in suffering. Opening more and more, we let go of the pain, the anger, the resentment, the blame, the sense of unfairness, the fear; we shift increasingly to the heart-center, becoming more and more deeply who we have always been: pure, open awareness filled with a love that ever makes room for what is present to present itself, a love that has no ax to grind and no conclusions to sell, a love that recognizes and delights in the miracle of being. When Moses asks God who He is, his remarkable question is met with a remarkable answer: "I AM THAT I AM." For the heart, this "I am" includes all else and therefore is always enough, while the willful-mind's "I am" excludes the heart and is therefore never enough. When we come to the "I" of "I am" that is not separate, we become as little children again.

Physically, we are many, but at heart, there is only the oneness of a miraculous, shared awareness that incomprehensibly encompasses all things, even those doing the sharing. Nothing can stand outside awareness, outside the heart. This means that in every essential way, living from the heart makes us aware of our greater identity in each moment. Though the mind perceives real differences, at heart we are the same. This single, unbroken heart of the world is the root chord of the collective human symphony, the one "I am" that hides from itself in separate minds and returns to itself in heartful awareness. Within the edgeless arena of this shared awareness is the fertile soil of art, through which we express and celebrate the world; of science, through which we understand it; of religion, through which we seek to comprehend its mysteries; and of love, through which we stretch beyond the cocoons of our little selves to discover, explore, express, understand, and celebrate something greater. The love that reaches out in this way from the single heart of the world is more than an emotion; it is a way of being that, by its willingness, allows life to be joyful and sufficient and is spontaneously competent to care for itself and others. Each person we encounter is somehow no longer separate from us and becomes, in the generosity of whole-hearted awareness, essential—like the rose or fox that Saint-Exupéry's Little Prince "tames." We can commune with the world heart-to-heart, celebrating both our common wellsprings and the endless diversity of all it presents, each day. Because the heart is naturally open to itself and others, because it loves what is real, loves to see and understand and accommodate and realize its oneness with what is real, it is watchful. Because it is watchful in this heartfelt way, it gains access to the miraculous vision Martin Buber describes in *I and Thou* as the "hallowing of the everyday." The heart's awakening reveals a world renewed. Suffering dissipates like a bad dream from which we have finally awakened, and we see the face of our own, loving awareness in all faces, in the face of a stranger walking along a dark campus at night. There, and everywhere else, the miracle is in place, and we see that there never was any such thing as a stranger.

THE BIGGER PICTURE

WITH ALL WE HAVE SAID about the self, we have only scratched the surface of the miracle of awareness. Clearly, the self we usually take ourselves to be—the willful-mind—is but the smallest part of who we are. As long as we are ignorant of that calm openness within which all thought, all feeling, all bodily sensations, all phenomena arise, peak, and pass away, our natural delight in clarity, spontaneous expression, wisdom, and love must remain a mere possibility. This openness is associated with generosity, fullness, clarity, like an open autumn sky. When we expand into this openness, our awareness is released from constriction and suffuses the vast, dimensionless horizon of consciousness in a way that is quite difficult to describe. This awareness has great integrity and may be experienced as unlimited place, a boundary-less embrace of all that is. It is the domain of the one heart we all share, of the self behind the self we think we are. Within it, separateness has no meaning because the self is no longer at war with itself.

Along the way to this awakening, we come to realize that who we are is in many ways given to us, that we cannot completely fashion ourselves along the lines of our desires. In fact, it is these very desires that keep us stuck, including the desire for our suffering to end. When we see that much of who we are is given to us, we recognize that we exist always in relation to something greater than our own will. Spiritually, we are all receivers, which is why it is said that the highest form of prayer asks only for awareness of God's will. As the heart witnesses itself in all things, it begins to receive clues, signposts, messages that have been left by its own greater identity to draw it increasingly out of its self-hiddenness into the light of more and more awareness and love. When we awaken to the reality that we are not entirely self-willed, trusting becomes an act of worship and openness a way of life.

This idea serves as the basis for programs like Alcoholics Anonymous, Al-Anon, and others for overcoming addiction, all of which place great emphasis on the idea of surrender to something greater than our little will. Because the addicted person suffers from "self-will run riot," surrender actually liberates him from self-destructive habit and empowers him to live more fully. Through surrender, the willful-mind learns to acknowledge its origins despite the fact that it cannot understand them. This is fundamental: The mind cannot fathom the true self. Surrender, at some point, is inevitable, even if only at the time of physical death. There is a teaching that says, "Learn to die before you die, and you will not die even when you die." This "death before death" is the surrender of the willful-mind to the something greater it cannot fathom.

Across every barrier of time and place, we find the idea expressed that human awareness contains greatness. The ancient Hindu text, the *Upanishads,* for example, declares that the individual soul is of the same essence as God. Christianity purports that "the Kingdom of Heaven is within you." Judaism's Hasidic tradition makes reference to the individual soul as a "spark of light," and so with the other spiritual paths of the world. There is universal recognition that the part contains the whole even though it cannot comprehend it, that the individual is, in essence, one with the reality it apprehends. The underlying unity of the self and the world, experienced by the heart as love, has nothing

to do with the shattered mirror of the willful-mind's fears, justifications, ideas of ownership, or thousand resistances that are its
restless vocation. In moments of genuine empathy with others,
we are closer to our real identity than we know. But given our
sleepwalking and the great emotional investment we make in our
delusions, we do not let this happen often. Dedicated to main-
taining its sense of separateness, the willful-mind keeps us embroiled in combat. Secretly, it wishes to believe there is nothing
greater than itself. It perceives empathy as dangerous and considers letting-go a moral cop-out. Once the mind falls into the heart,
however, we awaken to our genuine identity[1] and the war ends.
In proportion to our receptivity, we experience the oneness love
makes possible and real and, perhaps to our amazement, find we
are in love with or without a partner. This is why, ultimately, the
way out of the suffering of having lost a love is to find out who
we are and to come to realize that we can no more be abandoned
by love than waves can be abandoned by the ocean.

Fulfillment is a moment of completion, of returning home, and
we may even understand home as that place we always come back
to. Beneath its willfulness and forgetfulness, the mind knows its
origins reside in something greater than itself, that not having
created itself, it can never resolve the question of its identity and
cannot fulfill itself. This is why the mind is so defensive and
quick to contend. Though it will exhaust itself seeking to maintain the delusion of its separateness and primacy, it must eventually bow to the heart in order to end its self-imposed struggle,
transcend suffering, and wake up to the joy of its true, spacious
identity.

*As difficult as it may be to feel the truth of this when we have been left
by someone we love, we are not unloved.* Our very identity is love. We
have only forgotten how to pay attention to who we are. It is

---

[1]The word "genuine" comes from the Latin *genu*, meaning "knee," the reference here being to the tradition in which a father recognized his newborn child
by placing it on his knee. When something is genuine, it is recognized as belonging, as being in its proper place. Thus, our genuine identity is the identity within
which we most fully belong to ourselves. (See "Space and Place," pages 162–164.)

ironic that being left by someone can lead us to remember the love that can never abandon us, even though we continually fail to attend to it. Here, again, the etymology is revealing: "attend" comes from the Latin *tendere,* meaning "to stretch." When we pay attention, when we attend to something, we stretch ourselves, we expand, we open. Paying attention is an act that opens up a place for something to be recognized, acknowledged, appreciated. Paying attention is the act of caring through which we expand awareness, and our caring sets us upon the "celestial highway," written of by Plato, that leads us home.

In practical terms, we are free to live in "the bigger picture," which means we are free to take what happens in our outer life as an opportunity to become more aware of our inner life, to deepen heart-awareness. Thus, we step across the artificial barrier of "inner" and "outer" and simply cultivate heart-awareness by being willing to see into the heart of whatever is asking for our attention. Through this increasing willingness to enter the heart, we find our experience taking on a newfound richness and a symbolic significance not unlike that of dreams. This practice begins with the recognition that whatever carries an emotional "charge" for us does so because it speaks to our heart—in other words, because it has something to teach us about who we are. It is not an easy path to take; we are understandably reluctant to give up the willful-mind's comforts of blaming and judging others and assume this sort of unconditional responsibility in order to become more fully who we are. But once we become willing to embark upon the high path of the heart, we can discover tremendous joy.

What does it mean to take unconditional responsibility for whatever we encounter? It means we assume the role of student, unconditionally, that we examine whatever happens with one purpose in mind: to deepen and broaden heart-awareness. For example: Let us say I am driving along the expressway. I look in my rear view mirror and see a car tailgating mine at sixty miles an hour. I am incensed! How dare this idiot endanger my life! Here, he speeds along his way, oblivious to the fact that he is practically running right over me, and what does he care? When I react in this way, I am a victim of external conditions. Now, suppose I remember, in the heat of the moment, to make the shift to taking responsibility for what is happening. What does this driver have to teach me? Why am I bothered by him? The first thing I realize is that the tailgating situation is something we are both creating. Clearly, I could change lanes and end the problem. I become aware that I have my hand in the monkey trap, that I am contributing decisively to my own suffering, holding onto the very thing that is causing me pain. Opening further, I realize this man reminds me of myself, of my own ability to drive recklessly toward a goal without regard for consequences. How many arguments have I won by running over the feelings of others? Going deeper, I note how my willful-mind does not like to look in the mirror of these shortcomings; it prefers to deny them but ends up condemning in others what it has denied in itself, and this is why the situation is so annoying. (I am even seeing this fellow in a mirror.) Now, I have become aware of my own stubbornness and recklessness and, further, that I still wish to deny these, that I have not forgiven them in myself. How then, could I expect to forgive them in another? If I had taken these into my heart, I would simply get out of his way, without emotional entanglement. What is he to me, after all? And this is precisely the question for awareness. As long as he represents something about me I have denied, I will project that thing onto him and hate him for it. There will be an emotional resonance that demands my attention because it needs my attention. The practical result of using the situation as a way to gain deeper access to my own heart is that, whether this man knows it or not, he is my teacher. He makes me aware of my own stubbornness, recklessness, my unwillingness to forgive. In the moment that I expand my awareness to include this without judgment and become willing to love and accept it in myself, I am freed to experience it in him without judgment, free not to give it significance, free not to take it to heart. The emotional sting is gone because there is no longer a resonance. The heart has taken the mind's battle and transmuted it into deeper understanding. I pull over into the next lane and he whizzes by. Looking in the mirror again, I see an open road and notice the hint of a smile of gratitude.

It is possible to live this way, and no problem is ever without its gift. At first, it is difficult to remember, but our sense of purpose is rooted in the recognition that we are taking part in the most exciting adventure there is—the adventure of becoming who we are.

EPILOGUE: BEING ALIVE IS
BETTER THAN HEALING

IN THE COURSE of recovering from my own broken heart, I peeked behind the veil of lifelong habit and saw that, underneath the awful dramas that frighten and hurt us so, we humans are a kind of effervescence—learning, intending, acting upon, participating in this world that presents itself to us, somehow, as distinct from us, even while surrounding and permeating us, a fountain rising up out of the very water that forms it, different yet the same. I found comfort in this vision of interdependence because it implies that we are not condemned to be victims, passively reacting to our own thoughts, feelings, or worldly circumstances, though we may certainly play that role if we choose to. Choice is given, always, even if it is only the choice to refuse to give our attention. Choice is a responsibility, and choosing has its price; sometimes this price is extremely high, but we need never pay the price of being victims. Even in times of the seemingly greatest victimization and powerlessness, we may become aware, catch ourselves in the act of complicity, glimpse ourselves holding the brush, so to speak, and, most important, relax our grip and begin to paint something else.

After the storm of losing a loved one, the challenge is the same as it always was: to open to the goodness of life in its course, to allow its fullness even into our suffering. This challenge abides whether we have a partner or not, whether we decide to wait for reconciliation or not, whether we are willing to enter our heart and awaken to the profusion of the living present or remain closed even longer, deepening our grief rather than releasing it. Sometimes, the news that we are free to step out of suffering brings a certain sadness. Certainly, the loss of suffering itself is a loss, and an important one, for in it we lose a part of ourselves that has been with us for a long time. Many therapists have seen a patient reach the point at which he is sufficiently aware of his own addictive patterns to be able to throw them off and begin to live freely, only to see him balk, as it were, at the brink of freedom. It is all too much. The old patterns, even if painful, are familiar. And, as we have discussed, there are benefits to remaining within our private prisons. Freedom calls us to accept the unknown and therefore to take real risks. It means we cannot pretend we are still sleeping; if we are aware, we are responsible to live up to what we have seen. In this moment, there is a new kind of aloneness: We realize that no one will live our life for us. It is up to us to allow our life to be good, or to continue to resist our own inherent goodness by serving the willful-mind as our master. We see that we are *deeply* free—to accept or deny our own awareness, to decide, to choose, to act, to live, to walk out of the prison into the miracle of being richly, consciously alive. It is a formidable prospect.

If you are still inclined, despite all you have been through, to hide in bed with the covers pulled up over your head, this prospect will not sound inviting. You may feel that sitting quietly and paying attention to what you are really feeling, to how you may be holding onto your suffering simply requires too much: too much patience, too much perseverance, too much courage. Your heart hurts, and all you want is for things to be back to "normal," to be held by your former partner and told you are understood and loved, that it has all been a horrible mistake that is finally over. Anyone who has had a piece of his heart torn away feels like this for a while. Know that the pain will pass. The will to live and love will return. You will heal. And if, at that time, you are willing to acknowledge and honor the miracle that is your true self, you will find that your pain has broadened and deepened you, that it has somehow contributed to there being more of you. You will find that throwing off the constrictions of self-pity, impatience, and second pain, that living freely, is better than healing. Your carefully cultivated self-awareness and compassion will naturally expand to include a greater awareness of and compassion for others passing through similar storms. They will sense the calm strength of self-honesty and self-acceptance resonating in the depths of you and, recognizing their own spiritual possibility, may even approach you to discuss their problems and feelings. Having honestly witnessed and forgiven your addiction, having gone beyond mere reaction, you will find life more original, more exciting, richer. You will recognize that, all things considered, your suffering was as inevitable as the rain, and you will not have regrets. For this much is certain: No one who loves another would choose to lose that love in order to learn a lesson, no matter how great. But for those who lose a love and find the way back to their own heart, no lesson can be greater.